Managing Climate Risks and Impacts Through Due Diligence for Responsible Business Conduct

A TOOL FOR INSTITUTIONAL INVESTORS

OECD
BETTER POLICIES FOR BETTER LIVES

This document, as well as any data and map included herein, are without prejudice to the status of or sovereignty over any territory, to the delimitation of international frontiers and boundaries and to the name of any territory, city or area.

Please cite this publication as:
OECD (2023), *Managing Climate Risks and Impacts Through Due Diligence for Responsible Business Conduct: A Tool for Institutional Investors*, OECD Publishing, Paris, https://doi.org/10.1787/8aee4fce-en.

ISBN 978-92-64-39496-4 (print)
ISBN 978-92-64-92407-9 (pdf)
ISBN 978-92-64-75315-0 (HTML)
ISBN 978-92-64-63239-4 (epub)

Photo credits: Cover © Jupiterimages/Getty Images.

Corrigenda to OECD publications may be found on line at: www.oecd.org/about/publishing/corrigenda.htm.

Foreword

Climate change is the defining challenge of our time, requiring urgent, ambitious action from all global actors. Institutional investors in particular will play a vital role in enabling a transition to net zero by enabling the provision of financing toward products, services and technologies necessary for the transition and aligning their investments with temperature goals of the 2015 Paris Agreement.

In this context, this tool on *Managing Climate Risks and Impacts through Due Diligence for Responsible Business Conduct* (RBC) (the tool) aims to explain how the RBC due diligence framework can be applied by institutional investors to address adverse climate impacts associated with their investee companies, as understood under the OECD Guidelines for Multinational Enterprises on Responsible Business Conduct.

The tool also provides an initial overview of how the RBC due diligence framework relates to and can draw on other frameworks and tools for assessing, managing or disclosing climate-related impacts associated with their investments. In this respect, Annex A of this tool provides an overview of how the RBC due diligence framework compares with leading initiatives and disclosure frameworks used by investors with respect to climate impacts (e.g. the Task Force on Climate Related Financial Disclosures).

This tool does not intend to create new standards of conduct but rather to outline measures and practical actions investors can take to carry out RBC due diligence with respect to climate risks and impacts. The tool also discusses the potential value to investors in carrying out RBC due diligence in connection with other sustainability objectives (i.e. biodiversity and social).

This tool was produced by Barbara Bijelic and Benjamin Michel from the Centre for Responsible Business Conduct of the OECD's Directorate for Financial and Enterprise Affairs and by Géraldine Ang from the Finance, Investment and Global Relations division of the OECD's Environment Directorate. The report was developed under the direction of Allan Jorgensen, Head of the OECD Centre for Responsible Business Conduct. It benefited from valuable insights from Raphaël Jachnik and Jolien Noels (Environment Directorate). Communications support was provided by Thorfinnur Ómarsson and Zara Kuruneri.

The tool has been developed through close consultation with a multi-stakeholder advisory group of representatives from the financial sector, industry leaders, government, civil society, trade unions international organisations and other experts. This paper was approved by the OECD Working Party on Responsible Business Conduct in July 2023 and by the OECD Investment Committee and the OECD Environmental Policy Committee in September 2023.

This tool is part of the work the OECD undertakes to clarify expectations of responsible business conduct due diligence in the context of enterprises operating in the financial sector. The OECD has also developed tailored guidance to help enterprises carry out due diligence in other sectors, specifically: extractives, and particularly minerals from conflict affected and high-risk areas; garment and footwear; and agriculture.

Table of contents

FIGURES

TABLES

Executive summary

Achieving climate mitigation and adaptation goals of the Paris Agreement requires making finance consistent with a pathway towards low greenhouse gas emissions and climate-resilient development, as called for by Article 2.1.c of the agreement (UNFCCC, 2015[1]). This will necessitate that policy makers, standard setters and financial actors pay increased attention to the real-economy climate impacts of finance.

The *OECD Guidelines for Multinational Enterprises on Responsible Business Conduct* and related paper *Responsible Business Conduct for Institutional Investors* provides practical recommendations as to how investment managers and asset owners can undertake due diligence across their investee companies to identify and respond to environmental and social impacts, including climate change. Together they provide a comprehensive framework to understand institutional investor's relationship to climate risks and impacts, which are directly linked to their investments and activities (including through their ownership in, or management of, shares in an investee company or asset). From this specific framework flows a number of RBC due diligence expectations for how institutional can identify, prevent, mitigate and account for how they manage and disclose climate risks and impacts.

In particular, RBC due diligence for investors consists of six main steps or supporting measures, which provide concrete recommendations on how to:

1. Embed climate considerations into investor policies and management systems, as a necessary foundation for ensuring that climate risks and impacts are adequately identified and managed.
2. Identify and assess climate risks, impacts and opportunities in portfolio, at asset, asset class and sector levels, to inform investors about climate risks and impacts associated with their investee companies and thereby inform their strategy and prioritisation for responding to those risks.
3. Seek to prevent or mitigate actual or potential climate impacts, including through engagement, active ownership and stewardship; and by responding to climate considerations through portfolio allocation.
4. Track implementation and results of due diligence, both when it comes to their own performance against their policies (including objectives and targets related to climate), as well as investee companies' efforts in preventing and mitigating impacts.
5. Communicate how climate risks and impacts are addressed, as a way to demonstrate the level of ambition and effectiveness of an investor's due diligence process towards its stakeholders.
6. Encourage investees to provide for or co-operate in remediation when appropriate.

In addition, the tool draws on a number of key climate-related frameworks, coalitions and methodologies to highlight the synergies between the RBC due diligence framework and its above listed steps with existing or excepted practices by institutional investors when it comes to managing and disclosing climate risks and impacts.

Introduction

This chapter introduces the context, scope and rationale for the tool as well as how it builds on OECD standards and principles of Responsible Business Conduct and existing OECD work on ESG investing approaches.

The integration of climate-related risks and opportunities into investment strategies is gaining momentum among different types of institutional investors globally, driven by increased attention from regulators, changing market practices, and stakeholder expectations. Key trends include rising shareholder activism, increased investor engagement and policy initiatives (e.g. through the development of disclosure and governance requirements). Overall, this is leading to heightened expectations for institutional investors to consider adverse climate impacts that their investee companies and assets in their portfolios can have on society and the environment as well as on their financial performance.

In that context, institutional investors are increasingly adopting net zero commitments. However, studies have shown considerable variations as to the ways voluntary commitments materialise in practice and have raised concerns over the quality of commitments with regard to the credibility and transparency of their approaches (Noels and Jachnik, 2022[2]; OECD, 2017[3]). Grounding net-zero commitments in standards as highlighted by the UN High-Level Expert Group on the Net Zero can strengthen their credibility and comparability and level up the global playing fields among institutional investors (UN HLEG, 2022[4]).

Responsible business conduct standards, and in particular the *OECD Guidelines for Multinational Enterprises on Responsible Business Conduct* ("The *OECD Guidelines*") and related OECD due diligence guidance, lay out the expectation that business, including investors, avoid and address adverse impacts of their activities on society and the environment (including climate change), throughout their own activities and business relationships, by carrying out due diligence, while contributing to sustainable development. RBC due diligence is the process enterprises should carry out to identify, prevent, mitigate and account for how they address adverse risks and impacts in their own operations, their supply chains and other business relationships, as recommended in the *OECD Guidelines.* The RBC due diligence process is dynamic, ongoing and informed by stakeholder engagement (OECD, 2018[5]). The role of RBC in the context of climate change and other environmental challenges has become particularly pertinent in light of the climate crisis, as well as increasing expectations regarding mandatory and voluntary environmental supply chain due diligence (OECD, 2021[6]).

This tool provides an overview of practical actions and key considerations with respect to RBC due diligence approaches relevant for institutional investors i.e. institutional investment managers and asset owners, including commercial banks, mutual funds, pension funds, hedge funds, insurance companies. It does not outline specific approaches for entities that facilitate investment (e.g. market research providers, investment banks that provide research on listed companies and execute trades, underwrite new security issuance and provide research for initial public offerings, stock exchanges, index providers etc.). However, it may be a useful reference for these entities as well since the recommendations of the *OECD Guidelines* are also applicable to them.

Where relevant, the tool distinguishes between approaches that may be specifically relevant for asset owners and asset managers, as well as specific assets and asset classes. In practice, investors may use a combination of investment strategies and asset classes and the line between these categories may be blurred. In these situations, a combination of approaches may be used.

The OECD paper on *Responsible Business Conduct for Institutional Investors* provides practical recommendations as to how investment managers and asset owners can undertake due diligence across their investee companies to identify and respond to environmental and social impacts, including climate change, as defined under the *OECD Guidelines* (OECD, 2017[7]; OECD, 2023[8]) (see Overview of climate-related provisions in the *OECD Guidelines* and *Due Diligence Guidance* for more information). The tool further builds on analytical work undertaken by the OECD Directorate for Financial and Enterprises Affairs on ESG investing approaches among institutional investors, including among asset managers and asset owners, pension funds and insurance companies (Patalano, 2020[9]; OECD, 2017[3]).

Overview of climate-related provisions in the *OECD Guidelines* and *Due Diligence Guidance*

This chapter introduces the main climate-related provisions in the *OECD Guidelines* and *Due Diligence Guidance*. It defines the concepts of climate risks and impacts through the perspective of RBC principles and standards and how the concepts interact with other approaches (i.e. financial materiality and climate science). The chapter further outlines investor's relationship to climate risks and impacts.

Climate-related provisions under the OECD *Guidelines* and OECD *Due Diligence Guidance for Responsible Business Conduct*

The *OECD Guidelines for Multinational Enterprises on Responsible Business Conduct* ("the *OECD Guidelines*") are the most comprehensive government-backed instrument on Responsible Business Conduct (RBC) – covering all areas of business responsibility, including a dedicated chapter on the Environment, amongst others. The *OECD Guidelines* call on companies (including investors) to avoid causing or contributing to adverse impacts and seek to prevent or mitigate adverse impacts associated with their activities and business relationships. The *OECD Guidelines* also recognise that investors should contribute positively to environmental, economic, and social progress worldwide, with a view to achieving sustainable development (OECD, 2023[8]).

The Environment chapter of the *OECD Guidelines* provides a set of recommendations for enterprises, including investors, to ensure strong environmental performance and help minimise their contribution to negative environmental impacts.[1] It provides that enterprises should, *inter alia* (OECD, 2023[8]):

- *1. Establish and maintain a system of environmental management appropriate to the enterprise associated with the operations, products and services of the enterprise over their full life cycle, including by carrying out risk-based due diligence [...] for adverse environmental impacts [including climate change], including through:*
    - a) *identifying and assessing adverse environmental impacts associated with an enterprise's operations, products or services [...]*
    - b) *establishing and implementing measurable objectives, targets and strategies for addressing adverse environmental impacts associated with their operations, products and services and for improving environmental performance. Targets should be science-based, consistent with relevant national policies and international commitments, goals, and informed by best practice;*
    - c) *regularly verifying the effectiveness of strategies and monitoring progress toward environmental objectives and targets, and periodically reviewing the continued relevance of objectives, targets and strategies;*
    - d) *providing the public, workers, and other relevant stakeholders with adequate, measurable, verifiable (where applicable) and timely information on environmental impacts associated with their operations, products and services based on best available information, and progress against targets and objectives as described in paragraph 1.b;*
    - e) *providing for or co-operating in remediation as necessary to address adverse environmental impacts the enterprise has caused or contributed to and using leverage to influence other entities causing or contributing to adverse environmental impacts to remediate them. [...]*
- *5. Continually seek to improve environmental performance, at the level of the enterprise and, where appropriate, entities with which they have a business relationship."*

The commentary to Environment chapter of the *OECD Guidelines* further provides that:

- *76. Enterprises have an important role in contributing towards net- zero greenhouse gas emissions and a climate resilient economy, necessary for achieving internationally agreed goals on climate change mitigation and adaptation. During the process of transitioning to net-zero greenhouse gas emissions, many business activities will involve some level of emissions of greenhouse gases or reduction of carbon sinks. Enterprises should ensure that their greenhouse gas emissions and impact on carbon sinks are consistent with internationally agreed global temperature goals based on best available science, including as assessed by the Intergovernmental Panel on Climate Change (IPCC).*

- *77. This includes the introduction and implementation of science-based policies, strategies and transition plans on climate change mitigation and adaptation as well as adopting, implementing, monitoring and reporting on short, medium and long-term mitigation targets. These targets should be science-based, include absolute and also, where relevant, intensity-based GHG reduction targets and take into account scope 1, 2, and, to the extent possible based on best available information, scope 3 GHG emissions. It will be important to report against, review and update targets regularly in relation to their adequacy and relevance, based on the latest available scientific evidence and as different national or industry specific transition pathways are developed and updated. Enterprises should prioritise eliminating or reducing sources of emissions over offsetting, compensation, or neutralisation measures. Carbon credits, or offsets may be considered as a means to address unabated emissions as a last resort. Carbon credits or offsets should be of high environmental integrity and should not draw attention away from the need to reduce emissions and should not contribute to locking-in greenhouse gas intensive processes and infrastructures. Enterprises should report publicly on their reliance on, and relevant characteristics of, any carbon credits or offsets. Such reporting should be distinct from and complementary to reporting on emissions reduction.* […]
- *79. Achieving climate resilience and adaptation is a critical component of the long-term global response to climate change to protect people and ecosystems and will require the engagement and support of all segments of society. Enterprises should avoid activities, which undermine climate adaptation for, and resilience of, communities, workers and ecosystems."*

The *OECD Guidelines* call on enterprises to carry out risk-based due diligence to avoid and address adverse impacts on people, planet and society. RBC due diligence is understood as the process through which enterprises can "identify, prevent, mitigate and account for how they address their actual and potential adverse impacts as an integral part of business decision-making and risk management systems" (OECD, 2023[8]). Section II provides an overview of the key measures under the due diligence framework and how they can be adapted by institutional investors in the context of climate impacts.

Understanding climate impacts and risks under the OECD *Guidelines* and associated due diligence approach for investors

The *OECD Guidelines* and associated RBC due diligence guidances are concerned primarily with actual and potential adverse impacts on people and the planet associated with business activity:

- Under the *OECD Guidelines*, climate change is recognised as an **adverse environmental impact**, which itself is defined as "*significant changes in the environment or biota which have harmful effects on the composition, resilience, productivity or carrying capacity of natural and managed ecosystems, or on the operation of socio-economic systems or on people.*" (OECD, 2023[8]).
- Building on the *OECD Guidelines* definition, in the present tool, ***climate risks*** refer to the potentiality of such impacts arising. Unless otherwise specified, this is the meaning attributed to this term throughout this tool.

Climate impacts and risks may be understood differently by different communities, e.g. climate scientists and investors, based on different perspectives.

- For many investors, *climate risks* refer to the financial risks posed to portfolios as a result of climate-related physical, transition and other liability risks (see Box 1).
- From the perspective of climate science, *climate impacts* refer to the effects on natural and human systems of extreme weather and climate events related to climate change. And *climate risks* refer to the risks of such climate impacts occurring (IPCC, 2023[10]) (Box 2). There are two approaches

needed for policy makers, private actors and other stakeholders to respond to climate change and manage climate risks and impacts: mitigation and adaptation.

Given the difference in focus of the RBC due diligence approach, which is focused on preventing and mitigating adverse impacts on people and planet associated with business activity, it may differ from existing investor practices related to climate risk management as well as from existing disclosure or reporting frameworks that focus on climate-related financial risks i.e. the Task Force on Climate-related Financial Disclosures (TCFD) (see Annex Table 3) or the International Sustainability Standard Board (ISSB).

Box 1. Climate related risks from the perspective of financial materiality

In addition to climate risks and impacts on society and the environment, investors and other financial actors consider different types of climate risks that can affect portfolio performance and financial stability. These include:

- ***Physical risks***, i.e. the impacts on insurance liabilities and the value of financial assets, including damage to assets and operations arising from climate- and weather-related events, including indirect impacts across supply chains.
- ***Transition risks***, i.e. the financial risks and reassessment of the value of assets that could result from the process of adjustment towards a lower-carbon or climate-resilient economy, due to changes e.g. in policy, regulation, law, technology or markets. Key drivers of transition risks include technological shocks (e.g. rapid decrease of renewable power costs); policy and regulatory shocks (e.g. introduction of a carbon price or resilience requirements); sudden changes in "climate sentiments" of financial actors; market shifts due to innovation, disruption and changes in consumer preferences; reputational risks; and risks related to legal liability.

Source: Carney (2015[11]), Breaking the tragedy of the horizon – climate change and financial stability – speech by Mark Carney, www.bankofengland.co.uk/speech/2015/breaking-the-tragedy-of-the-horizon-climate-change-and-financial-stability; Monasterolo (2019[12]), Climate Change and the Financial System, ssrn.com/abstract=3479380

Moreover, there are often interdependencies and linkages between climate-related financial risks and those associated with adverse impacts to society and the environment. The *OECD Guidelines* recognise that environmental impacts can be considered financially material if they can reasonably be expected to influence an investor's assessment of an enterprise's value; timing and certainty of an enterprise's future cash flows or an investor's investment or voting decisions. The determination of which information is material may vary over time, and according to the local context, enterprise specific circumstances and jurisdictional requirements. Impacts that may not seem to be financially material but that are relevant to people, and the planet may be financially material for an enterprise at some point. Due diligence processes, as outlined in this tool, can be a useful means by which investors can ensure they are effectively identifying impacts and risks in a consistent and credible manner, including impacts and risks which may be, or which may become financially material. (OECD, 2023[8])

Box 2. Understanding climate risks and impacts from the perspective of climate science

From the perspective of climate science, *climate impacts* refer to the effects on natural and human systems of extreme weather and climate events and of climate change. *Climate risks*, i.e. the potential of climate impacts arising, refer to the potential for consequences where something of value is at stake and where the outcome is uncertain, and recognising the diversity of values. Climate change involves complex interactions and changing likelihoods of diverse impacts. The risk of climate impacts results from the interaction of climate hazards (including hazardous events and trends) with the vulnerability and exposure of human and natural systems (Figure 1). Changes in both the climate system and socio-economic processes including adaptation and mitigation are drivers of hazards, exposure, and vulnerability.

Figure 1. Assessing and managing the risks of climate change

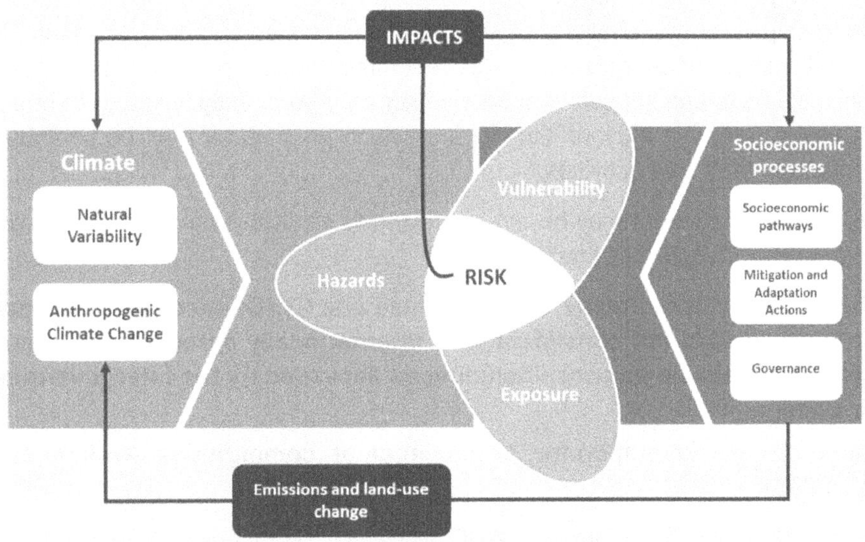

Source: Based on IPCC (2014[13]), *Impacts, Adaptation, and Vulnerability. Part A: Global and Sectoral Aspects. Contribution of Working Group II to the Fifth Assessment Report of the Intergovernmental Panel on Climate Change.* https://www.ipcc.ch/site/assets/uploads/2018/03/ar5_wgII_spm_en-1.pdf.

The severity and frequency of climate hazards materialise through both slow onset changes (e.g. in temperatures, precipitation patterns, sea level rise and biodiversity loss) and acute changes arising from particular events (e.g. weather-related events like floods, wildfires, drought, heatwaves, and the increasing frequency and severity of tropical storms). There is also the potential that critical thresholds in the climate system will be passed, triggering so-called tipping points that could have severe and irreversible impacts (e.g. collapse of the West Antarctic ice sheet, shut down of the North Atlantic Meridional Overturning Circulation).

Climate risks can cause significant socio-economic impacts (e.g. in terms of livelihoods, economic prosperity, development gains, ecosystem and human health, cultural losses, and possibly political stability and social coherence). Socio-economic impacts are further determined by a combination of exposure to the hazards, vulnerability and socio-economic resilience determining the ability to cope with and recover from disasters. Climate change can also have significant environmental impacts on itself, e.g. through threatening biodiversity, which underpins all life on land and below water, as well as ecosystem services delivered by biodiversity.

Source: IPCC, (2023[10]), AR6 Synthesis Report: Climate Change 2023, www.ipcc.ch/report/sixth-assessment-report-cycle; IIGCC, (2020[14]), Understanding physical climate risks and opportunities, www.iigcc.org; Lenton et al., (2008[15]), Tipping elements in the Earth's climate system, www.pnas.org/doi/full/10.1073/pnas.0705414105; Lenton et al., (2019[16]), Climate tipping points – too risky to bet against, www.nature.com/articles/d41586-019-03595-0; Hallegate et al., (2020[17]), From Poverty to Disaster and Back: a Review of the Literature, link.springer.com/article/10.1007/s41885-020-00060-5; OECD, (2022[18]), Climate Tipping Points: Insights for Effective Policy Action, doi.org/10.1787/abc5a69e-en.

Understanding investor's relationship to climate risks and impacts directly linked to their investments and activities

Under the *OECD Guidelines* and RBC due diligence framework, an investor's operations, products and services can be ***directly linked*** to climate risks and impacts through a business relationship, including through their ownership in, or management of, shares in an investee company or asset. This tool focuses on this type of relationship and therefore provides recommendations on carrying out RBC due diligence with respect to climate risks and impacts that an investor may be directly linked to through its assets and investee companies. It does not explore situations in which an investor may be contributing to adverse climate impacts through their own activities.[2]

In the context of this tool, investors may be *directly linked* to climate impacts and risks where they invest in assets or businesses with activities that:

- **Contribute directly or indirectly to greenhouse gas (GHG) emissions or impacts on carbon sinks in a way that is not consistent with internationally agreed global temperature goals based on best available science, including as assessed by the Intergovernmental Panel on Climate Change (IPCC)**; or
- **Undermine climate adaptation for, or resilience of, communities, workers and ecosystems** (OECD, 2023[8]).

During the process of transitioning to net-zero GHG emissions, many business activities will involve some level of emissions of GHG or reduction of carbon sinks. It will be important that investees introduce and implement strategies and transition plans on climate change mitigation and adaptation as well as adopt, implement, monitor and report on short-, medium- and long-term mitigation targets. These targets should be science-based, include absolute and also, where relevant, intensity-based GHG reduction targets and take into account scope 1, 2, and, to the extent possible based on best available information, scope 3 GHG emissions. (OECD, 2023[8])

For investors, it will be important that investment decisions at a transaction-level align with their own scope 3 targets and objectives.[3] (See Measure 4: Track implementation and results of due diligence for climate impacts for discussion on target and objective setting). Appropriate targets and objectives will vary across investors as well as with respect to assets and investee companies but should be consistent with a pathway towards low greenhouse gas emissions and holding the increase in the global average temperature to well below 2 °C above pre-industrial levels and pursuing efforts to limit the temperature increase to 1.5 °C above pre-industrial levels. It is important to recall that the expectation that investors seek to prevent or mitigate adverse climate impacts from their investments is not intended to shift responsibility from the investee company to prevent or mitigate its adverse climate impact itself. Investors are not generally responsible for the actions of the investee entity with which they have a business relationship, but rather for their own conduct, including their efforts to influence that entity.

In addition, this tool acknowledges that *how* investors seek to prevent and mitigate an adverse climate impact will depend on the type of asset class and investment strategy considered, the position in an investment portfolio, the mandate of the investor, their interpretation of investors duties, the type of investor (asset owner versus asset manager) as well as the regulatory context, as national circumstances differ (OECD, 2017[7]; 2017[3]). Institutional investors following the "Universal Owner" approach[4] for instance are more likely to take into account climate and other sustainability concerns compared to those engaged in traditional portfolio management (OECD, 2017[3]).

Box 3. Activities associated with adverse climate risks and impacts

Activities associated with adverse climate risks and impacts include:

a. ***Activities which are associated with GHG emissions or impacts on carbon sinks that are not consistent with the Paris Agreement temperature goal and based on best available science, including as assessed by the Intergovernmental Panel on Climate Change (IPCC)**:* Certain sectors, products, services or activities are associated with relatively higher levels of GHG emissions or reduction of carbon sinks and thus merit attention in the context of risk-based climate strategies and plans to finance and implement their transition. As recommended in the OECD Guidance on Transition Finance, to achieve the goals of the Paris Agreement, institutional investors can also play a key role in supporting high-carbon, energy-intensive, and hard-to-abate companies and economic activities transition to net-zero emission trajectories, and engagement with investee companies involved in such activities is encouraged to ensure real-economy decarbonisation. (OECD, 2022[19]) Such activities include but are not limited to:

    - **Activities in end-use sectors associated with significant GHG emissions**, including industry, transportation and building. For example, industrial production of materials (e.g. paper, cement or aluminium) or processing of commodities (e.g. use of cotton in garment and footwear sector) that result directly or indirectly in GHG emissions upstream in their supply chain, as well as land-use change.
    - **Activities associated with the generation, use and consumption of renewable or non-renewable energy** (e.g. extraction of resources, production, and transportation of fuel, and generation of electricity, steam, heating and cooling).
    - **Activities associated with the production of waste and pollutants that affect climate change** (OECD/CDSB, 2015[20]). For example, waste management generates methane, a GHG part of Short-Lived Climate Pollutants (SLCPs) generated by anaerobic waste decomposition in landfills (OECD, 2012[21]).
    - **Land use, land use change and forestry (LULUCF) and agriculture, and related GHG emissions** (CDSB, 2019[22]), including activities that negatively impact carbon sinks in terrestrial and marine environments, or activities that contribute to disturbance or destruction of wetlands, estuarine or tidal areas and coastal ecosystems such as mangroves.

b. ***Activities that may undermine climate adaptation for or resilience of communities, workers and ecosystems***: These are activities that fail to take into account climate resilience needs or lead to increased risks of negative impacts of climate change on people, the environment or other assets, or activities that hamper adaptation efforts. Examples include real estate or infrastructure in zones that are likely to be more exposed to flooding risk and other climate impacts and as such could eventually endanger human lives and livelihoods. In the case of infrastructure for instance, decisions on the location, design, operation and maintenance of infrastructure, as well as on their governance and financing, need to be assessed in relation to the exposure and vulnerability of infrastructure to a whole range of current and future climate risks, including flood protection, water supply, rainfall, extreme weather events and sea level rise.

Sources: European Commission, (2019[23]), Guidelines on reporting climate-related information, ec.europa.eu/info/files/190618-climate-related-information-reporting-guidelines_en; OECD and CDSB, (2015[20]), Climate change disclosure in G20 countries: Stocktaking of corporate reporting schemes, www.oecd.org/investment/corporate-climate-change-disclosure-report.htm; OECD, (2012[21]), Greenhouse gas emissions and the potential for mitigation from materials management within OECD countries, www.oecd.org/env/waste/50034735.pdf; CDSB, (2019[22]), CDSB Framework for reporting environmental and climate change information, www.cdsb.net/sites/default/files/climateguidancedoublepage.pdf.

RBC due diligence by institutional investors for climate risks and impacts

This chapter lays out the key steps and measures that institutional investors can take to carry out risk-based due diligence with respect to climate risks and impacts directly linked to their operations, products and services through a business relationship.

The structure of the chapter follows the key steps, supporting measures and associated recommendations as laid out by the OECD paper on *Responsible Business Conduct for Institutional Investors* (OECD, 2017[7])[5] and general guidance under the *OECD Due Diligence for Responsible Business Conduct* (OECD, 2018[5]) to provide asset owners and asset managers with the necessary tools to undertake risk-based due diligence with regards to climate risks and impacts directly linked to their operations, products and services through a business relationship.

In the context of climate risks and impacts directly linked to their activities by a business relationship, RBC due diligence for investors consists of six main steps or supporting measures (Figure 2):

1. **Embed climate considerations into investor policies and management systems, through:**
- Adopting policies on climate
- Embedding climate considerations into management systems through:
  - embedding climate considerations at a board level
  - embedding climate considerations at a management level
  - ensuring functional alignment
  - ensuring sufficient resources.
2. **Identifying and assessing climate risks, impacts and opportunities:**
- At portfolio-level
- Asset level, Asset-class or sectoral level
- Prioritising the most significant risks and impacts for further action.
3. **Seeking to prevent or mitigate actual or potential climate impacts, through:**
- Influencing existing assets and investees through engagement, active ownership and stewardship
- Portfolio allocation actions at asset-class or asset level, using available investment strategies
- Responding to climate considerations at portfolio-level.
4. **Track implementation and results of due diligence for climate impacts, through:**
- Developing objectives, targets and benchmarks to track climate performance at portfolio and asset level
- Tracking performance against those objectives, targets and benchmarks.
5. **Communicating how climate risks and impacts are addressed, through:**
- Publicly reporting relevant information on climate due diligence processes and their outcomes; and
- As relevant, communicating with stakeholders as to how climate risks and impacts are addressed.
6. **Encourage investees to provide for or co-operate in remediation when appropriate, through:**
- Encouraging investees to engage in restoration or take measures to prevent future climate impacts for example through adopting cleaner technologies or making changes to business models and activities.
- Encourage investees to provide for, or co-operate with, legitimate remediation mechanisms through which impacted stakeholders and rightsholders can raise complaints and seek to have them addressed.

Figure 2. RBC Due Diligence process and supporting measures applied to climate risks and impacts

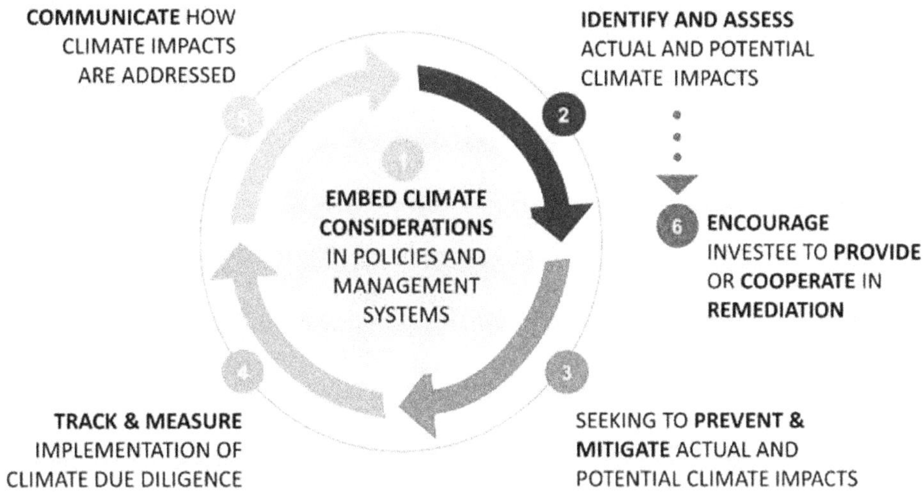

Source: Based on the OECD six-step framework on Due Diligence for RBC, OECD, (2018[5]), OECD Due Diligence Guidance for Responsible Business Conduct, https://mneguidelines.oecd.org/OECD-Due-Diligence-Guidance-for-Responsible-Business-Conduct.pdf.

This tool also outlines how OECD due diligence recommendations relate with existing frameworks and initiatives that investors are implementing to assess, manage and report on climate-related risks such as those outlined in Annex A.

Measure 1: Embed climate considerations into policies and management systems

Embedding climate considerations into policies and management systems provides the necessary foundation for ensuring that climate risks and impacts are adequately identified and managed. This measure involves 1) adopting policies on climate and 2) embedding climate into management systems. These are each discussed in turn below.

Adopting investor policies on climate

The *OECD Guidelines* call on enterprises, including investors, to introduce and implement science-based policies, strategies and transition plans on climate change mitigation and adaptation and adopt, implement, monitor and report on short-, medium- and long-term mitigation targets. These targets should be science-based, include absolute and also, where relevant, intensity-based GHG reduction targets and take into account scope 1, 2, and, to the extent possible based on best available information, scope 3 GHG emissions (OECD, 2023[8]). The RBC due diligence approach calls for enterprises to adopt policies that articulate its commitments to the principles and standards contained in the *OECD Guidelines* and its plans for implementing due diligence. (OECD, 2018[5]) In this respect, investors can adopt climate policies under which they commit to relevant international standards and agreements on climate such as the Paris Agreement,[6] set climate objectives and targets, in line with the outlined expectations, and articulate their approach to implementing climate due diligence.

This may involve the following practical actions:

- **Making climate objectives a policy objective,** including as part of investor-led initiatives. Investors can adopt climate objectives as part of their policies in line with their own countries or regions' climate mitigation objectives[7] and broader well-being goals,[8] as well as existing science-based initiatives. For example the Paris Aligned Investment Initiative (PAII), which explores how investors can align their portfolios with the goals of the Paris Agreement (including through a Net Zero Investment Framework), and the Net-Zero Asset Owner Alliance (NZAOA) which all seek to align portfolios with a 1.5 °C scenario and transition portfolios to net-zero GHG emissions by 2050 (IIGCC, 2020[24]; UNEP FI/PRI, 2020[25]). Investors can also adopt climate resilience and adaptation goals. (WBCSD, 2019[26]; IIGCC, 2022[27]).
- **Setting climate objectives and targets at portfolio, asset-class, key-sector and asset level** (IIGCC, 2020[24]; NZAOA, 2022[28]; SBTi, 2021[29]) (See sub-section on targets and metrics under Measure Developing objectives, targets and benchmarks to track climate performance at portfolio, asset-class and asset level. Track implementation and results).[9] This includes setting sub-portfolios targets for each key asset class, including listed equities, publicly traded corporate bonds, infrastructure and real estate, as well as sovereign debt, taking into account outstanding carbon footprint accounting challenges for sovereign debt (Noels and Jachnik, 2022[2]; NZAOA, 2022[28]). This also includes setting sector targets in key high-emitting sectors, e.g. oil and gas; utilities; transport; materials; agriculture, forestry and fisheries; chemicals; construction and buildings; and textiles (NZAOA, 2022[28]). As discussed under Measure 3: Seeking to prevent and mitigate actual and potential adverse climate impacts, investors may also adopt engagement targets (NZAOA, 2022[28]).
- **Incorporating climate considerations into "investment beliefs statements"** and broader sets of policies, assumptions and objectives that constitute investment governance[10] (e.g. for asset owners), and publishing responsible investment charters incorporating climate considerations (UN PRI, 2016[30]).
- **Addressing trade-offs and fostering synergies and co-benefits with other sustainability objectives**. When setting and implementing their climate policies, investors should seek to ensure consistency of climate policies with other environmental (e.g. biodiversity conservation and sustainable use) and social goals (e.g. human rights and well-being). This may allow investors to better understand the relationship between climate and other sustainability issues, while avoiding unintended adverse impacts (e.g. trade-offs with biodiversity objectives for some low-carbon land-use projects, as well as synergies and trade-offs between climate change mitigation and adaptation). In addition to addressing trade-offs, investors should try to foster synergies and co-benefits with other sustainability objectives, e.g. between biodiversity and climate change. Taking a more holistic approach across environmental goals can offer opportunities to harness synergies. Investing in protection, sustainable management and restoration of natural and semi-natural ecosystems, for example, could benefit biodiversity, while also reducing a company's carbon footprint and enhancing environmental resilience. Ensuring ongoing provision of key ecosystem services under a changing climate is particularly relevant.
- **Adopting a natural capital approach in decision-making** can help to understand and manage interdependencies between climate change, biodiversity and other sustainability objectives, thereby facilitating management of trade-offs and harnessing synergies. As discussed briefly under Measure 2: Identify and assess actual and potential adverse climate impacts, various tools and emerging measurement approaches are available to support natural capital accounting[11] (OECD, 2019[31]).

Embedding climate considerations into management systems

This sub-measure involves 1) embedding climate considerations at board level and 2) at management-level; 3) ensuring functional alignment and 4) ensuring sufficient resources allocation.

Embedding climate considerations at board-level

Without prejudice to their legal obligations, including in the context of corporate governance frameworks, regulatory obligations and fiduciary duties, **the board and executive committees of institutional investors should integrate climate considerations in their governance and strengthen their board and executive committees' oversight of material climate considerations** (Box 4).

This may involve the following practical actions:

- **Ensuring the board is accountable** for the investor's long-term resilience and adverse climate impacts and risks to society and the planet (WEF, 2019[32]).
- **Ensuring the composition of the board is sufficiently diverse in skills, knowledge and experience** relevant to climate change.
- **Embedding climate considerations in the board and committee structures**. This can include embedding climate considerations in existing committees or creating a dedicated climate (and sustainability) advisory committee with internal and external experts; ensuring material climate factors are discussed by relevant committees in charge e.g. of risk, audit, nomination or remuneration; and ensuring effective interaction with the executive management (e.g. with the Chief Risk Officer if climate is embedded in the risk committee) (WEF, 2019[32]).
- **Adjusting and clarifying the process and frequency by which the board and executive committees are informed about climate considerations**, and whether the board and executive committees consider climate considerations when reviewing and guiding strategy, major plans of action, risk management policies, annual budgets, business plans, the organisation's performance objectives and performance monitoring. (TCFD, 2017[33])
- **Aligning the executive incentive structure** to promote long-term value creation and goals of the investors, e.g. by including climate targets and indicators in the executive incentive schemes, where appropriate (WEF, 2019[32]).

Embedding climate considerations at management-level

It will be important that investors embed climate considerations (including adverse impacts, risks and opportunities) into management responsibilities.

This may involve the following practical actions:

- **Assigning climate-related responsibilities to executive and management-level positions or committees** and clarifying management's role in addressing and managing climate considerations, including in reporting to boards (TCFD, 2017[33]) (see Annex A).
- **Adjusting and clarifying associated organisational structures and processes** by which management is informed about climate-related considerations, and how management (e.g. through specific positions or management committees) monitors climate considerations (TCFD, 2017[33]).
- **Creating incentives for management to address climate considerations,** e.g. by adjusting the remuneration structure of management at group level or within investment managers.

Box 4. Expectations around assigning climate responsibilities to management and boards under OECD instruments

The *OECD Guidelines* recommend that enterprises apply good corporate governance practices drawn from the *G20/OECD Principles of Corporate Governance*. The *G20/OECD Principles of Corporate Governance*, the global standard for assessing and improving corporate governance frameworks, were revised in 2023, notably to include a new chapter on Sustainability and Resilience. The main goal of the chapter is for policy makers to provide incentives for companies and their investors to make decisions and manage their risks, in a way that contributes to the sustainability and resilience of the company. It recognises that the "corporate governance framework should ensure that boards adequately consider material sustainability risks and opportunities when fulfilling their key functions in reviewing, monitoring and guiding governance practices, disclosure, strategy, risk management and internal control systems, including with respect to climate-related physical and transition risks."

Other OECD instruments recognise the importance of integrating environmental risks in the governance of institutional investors. The *G20/OECD High-level Principles on Long-Term Investment Financing by Institutional Investors* stress the importance of integrating long-term environmental, social and governance (ESG) risks in the governance of institutional investors. The "governing body of an institutional investor should ensure that the institution can properly identify, measure, monitor, and manage the risks associated with long-term assets as well as any long-term risks – including environmental, social and governance risks – that may affect their portfolios".

Sources: OECD, (2023[8]), OECD Guidelines for Multinational Enterprises, doi.org/10.1787/9789264115415-en; OECD (2023[34]), G20/OECD Principles of Corporate Governance, doi.org/10.1787/9789264236882-en; OECD, (2013[35]), G20/OECD high-level principles of long-term investment financing by institutional investors, www.oecd.org/finance/private-pensions/G20-OECD-Principles-LTI-Financing.pdf.

Ensuring functional alignment

It will be important that investors ensure that responsibility for implementing aspects of climate policies are assigned across relevant roles and departments. This may involve the following practical actions:

- **Requiring co-ordination at group level to integrate climate considerations** across teams and processes (e.g. group investment officers, local investment managers, corporate responsibility teams, risk management and, if relevant, asset management affiliates) and clarifying that assessing and addressing climate considerations extends beyond the remit of sustainability departments to include core business functions (WBCSD, 2019[26]).
- **Clarifying and clearly defining linkages between climate and other sustainability or RBC responsibilities of management and processes,** to break silos between different objectives of management and optimise expertise and knowledge sharing.
- **Ensuring that climate policy is applicable to all investment managers**, both internal and external.
- **Engaging with internal investment advisors and managers and external managers** to understand whether and how they assess, manage and report on adverse climate considerations (including adverse impacts, risks and opportunities) in their investment and corporate engagement strategies and to provide training where necessary to ensure climate considerations are appropriately taken into account.
- **Incorporating climate considerations in investment mandates,** e.g. issued by asset owners for asset managers in the selection process of investment managers or the revision process of existing mandates, to promote climate risk management and avoidance of greenwashing (OECD, 2020[36]).

Providing sufficient resources to achieve commitments

It will be important that investors provide adequate resources commensurate with the extent of due diligence needed with respect to climate impacts.

This may involve the following practical actions:

- **Embedding climate considerations into strategic and financial planning processes** across relevant time periods, including short-, mid- and long-term, with actual timelines to match climate targets (e.g. 2030) (TCFD, 2017[33]).
- **Providing adequate support and resources** across all relevant departments (e.g. analysis, research and data gathering, investment management, corporate reporting, etc.), including by appointing climate experts to build climate expertise across relevant departments or relying on external resources.

Measure 2: Identify and assess actual and potential adverse climate impacts

In the context of RBC due diligence, identification and assessment are conducted to help inform investors about climate risks and impacts associated with their investee companies and thereby inform their strategy on how to seek to prevent or mitigate those risks and impacts, while helping them take advantage of any opportunities associated with climate issues. In this respect, as discussed, investors need to understand to what extent the activities of their (existing or potential) investee companies and assets under portfolios: a) are associated with GHG emissions or with reducing carbon sinks in a way that is not consistent with a pathway towards low GHG emissions; or b) do not take into account adaptation needs or undermine climate resilient development.

In addition to establishing the appropriate governance and management systems (See Measure 1: Embed climate considerations into policies and management systems), investors should also integrate climate assessment into portfolio screening and existing investment decision-making processes. This measure involves: 1) identifying and assessing climate risks, impacts and opportunities at asset, asset-class and sectoral level, 2) at portfolio level and 3) prioritising the most significant risks and impacts for further action.

Identifying and assessing climate risks, impacts and opportunities at asset, asset-class and sector levels

Investors should identify and assess existing and potential assets with respect to climate risks and impacts. Taking a risk-based approach means prioritising assets that a) most significantly contribute to high or increasing GHG emissions or to reducing carbon sinks and that are not effectively implementing science-based policies, strategies and transition plans on climate change mitigation or b) that undermine adaptation of and resilience to climate change of communities, workers and ecosystems.

To assess asset-level climate impacts and risks, investors typically need to assess scope 1, 2 and material scope 3 emissions associated with individual assets in their portfolios, e.g. based on GHG protocol accounting methodologies (IIGCC, 2021[37]; PCAF, 2022[38]); (see also Measure 4: Track implementation and results of due diligence for climate impacts).

Various practical tools exist for evaluating these impacts at asset-class level. As identified by OECD research (Noels and Jachnik, 2022[2]), the majority of tools focus on listed equity or corporate fixed income, and fewer address other asset classes. Examples include:

- Various existing climate-related assessments or scoring methodologies of issuers or benchmarks for **listed equity or corporate fixed income**. Existing tools include notably: the Transition Pathways Initiative (TPI) tool (Transition Pathway Initiative, 2021[39]); S&P Sustainable1 (formerly

Trucost) Paris Alignment (S&P Global, 2021[40]); Carbon 4 Finance Carbon Impact Analytics (CIA) (Carbon 4, 2021[41]); CDP-WWF Temperature Ratings (CDP/WWF, 2021[42]); MSCI Implied Temperature Rise (MSCI, 2021[43]); climate-related benchmarks produced by investor coalitions or international initiatives, such as the Net-Zero Company Benchmark of Climate Action 100+ initiative (Climate Action 100+, 2020[44]) or **sector-specific** benchmarks of automotive and electric utility companies by the World Benchmarking Alliance (World Benchmarking Alliance, 2021[45]); and climate benchmarks of credit ratings agencies and benchmark providers.

- Country-level tools for **sovereign bonds**. For instance, the Climate Change Performance Index (CCPI), published by Germanwatch, CAN International and the NewClimate Institute, evaluates the climate protection performance of 57 countries and the EU (Germanwatch, 2021[46]; IIGCC, 2020[24]);. Other tools include FTSE x Beyond Ratings' method (FTSE Russell, 2021[47]); Ninety One Net Zero Sovereign Index (Ninety One, 2021[48]); or the Climate Action Tracker (Climate Action Tracker, 2023[49]).
- The Carbon Risk Real Estate Monitor (CRREM) for **real estate** (CRREM, 2021[50]; IIGCC, 2020[24]).
- Increasingly, tools are also being developed for **private equity**. The Institutional Investors Group on Climate Change (IIGCC) has just launched a new private equity component for the Net Zero Investment Framework (NZIF) to help general partners (GPs) make and implement net zero commitments and allow limited partners (LPs) to incorporate private equity in net zero strategies for multi-asset portfolios (IIGCC, 2022[51]). MSCI is also building an alignment methodology for private equity and debt in collaboration with Burgiss Data (MSCI, 2021[52]).

In addition, several tools exist **to screen economic activities or sectors** associated with high GHG emissions or adverse climate impacts in terms of climate adaptation, which may or may not be relevant or usable at asset level. Investors can, for instance, use screening tools from credit ratings agencies to identify sectors associated with high GHG emissions, such as Moody's heat maps of sectors with high or very high exposure to carbon risk (Moody's Investors Service, 2016[53]).

The NZIF of IIGCC's Paris Alignment Investment Initiative (PAII) uses the NACE classification codes to identify "material" sectors in terms of mitigation (namely, those in NACE code categories A-H and J-L) (IIGCC, 2020[24]). Similarly, the EU Taxonomy (Box 6) also uses NACE codes (supplemented by CEPA and CReMA statistical classifications for environmental activities) to identify economic activities for which technical screening criteria were developed, and prioritise sectors responsible for 93.5% of direct GHG emissions in the EU (European Commission, 2019[54]). The NZAOA's Target Setting Protocol uses the NACE, GICS and BIC classification codes to set targets across "material" sectors (NZAOA, 2022[28]).

Box 5. Screening process to assess climate physical impacts and adaptation needs

Assessing assets for **climate adaptation and resilience** factors is particularly relevant for key sectors exposed to current and future climate physical risks, such as real estate and infrastructure assets. Screening portfolios to determine risky assets in this respect needs to be sector specific and to also consider local or regional geographical conditions.

Asset-level assessment is particularly relevant for adverse climate impacts and risks from a climate resilience or adaptation perspective. An increasing number of investors are considering systematic screening for exposure to physical climate risks, from a financial materiality perspective. Given that these risks will be location-specific, the assessment needs to be done at the level of the physical asset, rather than at an entity level. In this respect, the IIGCC has developed guidance for institutional investors to identify and understand physical climate risks. Though it targets financial-related physical risks, it may likewise be helpful to investors in assessing potential impacts on people and the environment. The guidance includes case studies to illustrate how investors can seek to understand how potential climate physical risks and resilience opportunities are taken into account in asset development, management and planning and to develop screening criteria to identify at risk assets.

However, additional work is necessary to establish comprehensive and useful metrics for adaptation across economic activities and underlying assets. Unlike climate mitigation, which can be captured with a single carbon footprint metrics, resilience and adaptation indicators are typically diffuse and complex Current metrics do not assess the corporate contribution to adaptation the same way that the mitigation metrics assess the corporate contribution to mitigation. The EU Taxonomy, for instance, had to adapt a process-based approach to adaptation, unlike for climate mitigation. Instead of searching for a single adaptation metric, new work is also needed to create sets of adaptation metrics usable by investors that can provide some comparability and standardisation, thus complementing context-specific metric.

Sources: IIGCC, (2020[14]), Understanding physical climate risks and opportunities, www.iigcc.org; OECD, (2018[55]), Climate Resilient Infrastructure, doi.org/10.1787/4fdf9eaf-en; S&P Global, (2021[40]), Climate Change Physical Risk dataset, www.marketplace.spglobal.com/en/datasets/trucost-paris-alignment-(186); Leiter and Olhoff, (2019[56]), Adaptation metrics – Current Landscape and Evolving Practices, www.researchgate.net/publication/336135027_Adaptation_metrics_-_Current_Landscape_and_Evolving_Practices.

Presently, many investors rely on ESG ratings and indexes as a proxy for assessing environmental (and social) performance of assets or portfolios, including with respect to climate considerations. While such tools can be useful, it is important to recognise that rapid growth in ESG investment has led to a proliferation of disclosure frameworks, metrics, rating methodologies and investment approaches on ESG issues (Patalano, 2020[9]; OECD, 2017[3]). In that regard, OECD research suggests that significant discrepancies may exist with respect to how rating agencies assess climate performance both from a financial and environmental integrity perspectives (Boffo et al., 2020[57]). As such, when using third party assessments and ratings, investors should ensure that methodologies applied are consistent with their own climate policies and objectives. Third party assessments and ratings can be used to inform investors' due diligence processes but should not be used as proxy or in place of those processes.

In addition to climate impacts, it will also be important for investors to identify investment opportunities that can positively contribute to climate objectives. In this regard, frameworks such as the EU Taxonomy can help identify and prioritise assets in real economic activities that contribute substantially to climate mitigation or adaptation objectives (European Union, 2020[58]).[12] In order for investors to positively contribute to sustainable development, it is also important to identify available investment pathways by asset class in productive assets and economic activities that support climate objectives (e.g. in electric vehicles, renewable power, energy efficiency, nature-based solutions, etc.).

Box 6. The EU Taxonomy Regulation on Sustainable Economic Activities

A number of countries have created official definitions of sustainable finance as well as more comprehensive classification systems, referred to as sustainable finance taxonomies. Taxonomies answer a need for greater certainty on the environmental sustainability of different types of investments.

For example, the EU Taxonomy Regulation, which entered into force in July 2020, aims to establish criteria for environmentally sustainable economic activities. The majority of economic activities covered in the EU Taxonomy Regulation have technical screening criteria to demonstrate a substantial contribution to climate change mitigation. These are accompanied by technical screening criteria for avoiding significant harm related to climate adaptation (along with four other environmental objectives).

The EU Taxonomy Regulation also includes social safeguards to be implemented to ensure that environmentally sustainable economic activities also align with the *OECD Guidelines* and the *UN Guiding Principles on Business and Human Rights*, the eight fundamental conventions identified in the *Declaration of the International Labour Organization on Fundamental Principles and Rights at Work* and the *International Bill of Human Rights*. The EU Platform on Sustainable Finance has advised that the application of the minimum safeguards should be considered aligned when adequately conducting risk-based due diligence on human rights and other social and governance risks and impacts.

Sources: EU TEG, (2020[59]), Taxonomy: Final report of the Technical Expert Group on Sustainable Finance, ec.europa.eu/info/sites/info/files/business_economy_euro/banking_and_finance/documents/200309-sustainable-finance-teg-final-report-taxonomy_en.pdf; European Commission, (2019[54]), EU taxonomy for sustainable activities, ec.europa.eu/info/publications/sustainable-finance-teg-taxonomy_en; OECD (2020[60]), Developing Sustainable Finance Definitions and Taxonomies, doi.org/10.1787/134a2dbe-en; EU Platform on Sustainable Finance, (2022[61]), Final Report on Minimum Safeguards, finance.ec.europa.eu/system/files/2022-10/221011-sustainable-finance-platform-finance-report-minimum-safeguards_en.pdf; Tandon, (2021[62]),Transition finance: Investigating the state of play: A stocktake of emerging approaches and financial instruments, doi.org/10.1787/68becf35-en.

Identifying and assessing climate risks, impacts and opportunities at portfolio level

Identifying and assessing climate risks, impacts and opportunities at portfolio level will be necessary for investors to understand their own scope 3 emissions as well as to track alignment with relevant climate targets and benchmarks overtime (for investors who have adopted such targets or objectives). Even for investors which have not set portfolio level climate targets, tracking portfolio level climate risks and impacts can help them to assess the effectiveness of their due diligence processes. (See also Measure 1: Embed climate considerations into policies and management systems and Measure 4: Track implementation and results of due diligence for climate impacts). This portfolio-level impact can be measured through various carbon footprinting metrics (see Measure 4: Track implementation and results of due diligence for climate impacts), as well as forward-looking analysis (Box 7).

Under an RBC due diligence approach, investors are expected to identify both actual (existing) as well as potential (future expected and projected) climate impacts and risks. This may involve the following practical actions:

- **Estimating the carbon footprint and other GHG emissions footprint of portfolios** across asset classes and investment types, using real or estimated data for all GHGs,[13] in line with TCFD recommendations and using appropriate metrics (see Measure 4: Track implementation and results of due diligence for climate impacts) (TCFD, 2017[33]).[14]
- **Identifying and assessing future expected and projected climate impacts and risks**. This requires:

- Setting the relevant short-, medium- and long-term time horizons. In this respect investment managers (and broader management) should seek to identify climate risks and impacts resulting from investment decisions, which take into account the useful life of underlying assets or infrastructure and the fact that climate risks and impacts typically manifest themselves over the mid- to long-term (TCFD, 2017[33]).
- Grounding identification and assessment efforts not just based on backward-looking metrics (such as carbon footprint) but also using **forward-looking** approaches such as **climate scenario analysis and climate stress tests** to assess climate risks, impacts and alignment with climate objectives of targets at portfolio or asset-class level (Box 7). As highlighted by OECD research, aggregate-level assessments at the level of financial portfolios add a layer of complexity compared to assessments at the level of individual assets and asset classes. As such portfolio-level metrics can both lack transparency and hide individual activities that may be misaligned (Noels and Jachnik, 2022[2])

- **Addressing possible trade-offs and fostering synergies with other environmental and sustainability goals**. As discussed previously under Measure 1: Embed climate considerations into policies and management systems, adopting a natural accounting approach can enable investors to foster synergies between climate, biodiversity and other environmental issues. Several emerging accounting approaches and methodologies are available to assess biodiversity-or nature-related impacts as well as dependencies in portfolios (OECD, 2019[31]; TNFD, 2023[63]);.

From a climate resilience and adaptation perspective, portfolio-level assessment may be less relevant than from a climate mitigation one. Nonetheless, a reasonable level of due diligence for possible climate impacts and risks from a climate resilience and adaptation perspective can be useful. In this respect, systematic screening e.g. for negative social impacts associated with climate resilience across investment decisions may be relevant to encourage climate risks to be managed by the investee company or the investor during the lifetime of the owning of the asset.

Prioritising the most significant climate impacts

Under the *OECD Guidelines*, investors are called on to prioritise identified adverse impacts and risks based on their **severity** and **likelihood**. Severity is assessed based on the scale (gravity of the impact), scope (reach of the impact) and irremediable character of the impact.

When prioritising across investee companies and assets on the basis of the severity of actual or potential climate impacts related to GHG emissions, investors may focus primarily on scale, meaning the volume and potency of GHG emissions or scale of reduced carbon sinks. As climate impacts are highly diffuse, their scope and irremediable character may be relatively equivalent across assets. In this respect:

- In terms of adverse impacts and risks for climate mitigation, investors may initially **prioritise assets and sectors associated with activities that investors assess to be associated with the most significant adverse climate impacts,** for example high GHG emitting sectors or key sectors to reducing carbon sinks, based on available metrics, indicators, sectoral classifications and screening tools (See above). The Net Zero Asset Owner Alliance has for instance identified the following priority, high emitting sectors: oil and gas; utilities, including coal; transport; materials, including steel, cement and aluminium; agriculture, forestry and fisheries; chemicals; construction and buildings; water utilities; textile and leather. Investors may also consider the lifecycle of assets and prioritise those which may be at risk of lock-in with respect to adverse climate impacts over the long term. In order to further prioritise assets or investee companies for the purposes of prevention and mitigation activities, investors should also assess to what extent these assets of investee companies have introduced and implemented science-based policies, strategies and transition plans on climate change mitigation and adaptation, as an indication of the future expected alignment trajectory.

- In terms of adverse impacts and risks for climate adaptation and resilience, **investors can prioritise identification and further due diligence measures for assets and sectors on the basis of the severity of climate impacts most likely to result in harm to people or the planet if investors fail to account for vulnerabilities or exposure to climate hazards in their investments.** Key priority sectors include large-scale infrastructure, real estate developments, energy and agricultural assets. Additional analysis however is needed to improve metrics for adaptation and understand which adaptation metrics and assessment tools are informative (see Measure 4: Track implementation and results of due diligence for climate impacts).

Importantly, prioritisation will often not be an exact science and companies have flexibility and ability to make judgement calls when making prioritisation decisions. However, investors should draw on science-based approaches and independent and accepted definitions of priority sectors for climate mitigation, e.g. high GHG emitting sectors. Consulting with stakeholders (e.g. asset managers or asset owners) on prioritisation decisions can help to ensure that prioritisation processes are credible and well informed.

Assets identified as most significant in terms of severity and likelihood of climate impacts under an RBC due diligence framework may be different to those identified through a framework assessing financially material climate impacts. For example, certain carbon-intensive assets (e.g. airline companies) may not yet be considered to be at high transition risk, yet they can be associated with significant adverse climate impacts. As a consequence, an RBC due diligence approach can enhance a financial-related risk-based approach (i.e. the TCFD framework) by enabling and fostering more forward-looking and broader-based due diligence. The RBC due diligence approach recognises a range of actions investors can take to seek to prevent and mitigate climate impacts. These are discussed under Measure 3: Seeking to prevent and mitigate actual and potential adverse climate impacts.

Importantly, **identifying and prioritising adverse climate impacts and risks at portfolio-level may require investors to consider potential trade-offs and benefits with other environmental and social goals considered in their investor policies**, such as biodiversity goals as well as human rights. The EU taxonomy interlinks environmental objectives through the multi-dimensional "Do No Significant Harm" (DNSH) requirement. In order to address social issues associated with climate transition, and support a "just transition", investors can consider applying a risk-based approach to their climate mitigation goals (OECD, 2019[64]). This is because the synergies between climate mitigation and other human rights and well-being goals can be leveraged around jobs, income, health, education and wider environmental quality (OECD, 2019[64]). Trade-offs between climate and other environmental and social goals cannot always be avoided but carrying out due diligence to identify the range of potential risks included under the *OECD Guidelines* (including human rights and labour issues) can help to identify and assess and to understand the best mitigation options (OECD, 2019[64]).

Responding to data, methodological and modelling challenges under an RBC approach

Despite the broad range of existing and emerging tools and methodologies available for investors to identify adverse climate impacts, risks and opportunities, investors face outstanding data, methodological and modelling challenges, to accurately identifying and assessing climate risks and impacts.

Availability, comparability, consistency and reliability of data and metrics

Investors currently lack commonly accepted methodologies, definitions and benchmarks to calculate carbon footprint and other climate metrics. Furthermore, investors often lack access to granular and comparable data on underlying assets needed to undertake climate assessment, particularly for non-listed companies. For example, the most commonly used metrics by financial institutions – carbon footprint or weighted average carbon intensity (See Measure 4: Track implementation and results of due diligence for climate impacts) – are generally limited to scope 1 and 2 emissions. Yet, depending on the real economy sector considered, scope 3 emissions may represent the majority of an entity's GHG emissions – in some cases up to 90%. (CDP, 2023[65]) There are however outstanding analytical gaps to identify and measure or estimate scope 3 emissions, in addition to double counting challenges (IIGCC, 2020[24]), and other attribution issues when it comes to scope 3 emissions reductions (ERCST, 2021[66]). To support investors, policy makers and broader society in tracking and monitoring real-economy impacts of financial sector commitments toward net-zero, a number of international initiatives (e.g. Net-Zero Data Public Utility) have been set up to foster more consistent and comparable metrics. (NZDPU, 2022[67])

Uncertainties with climate science and modelling

Investors also face uncertainties associated with the design and use of climate science and modelling. Investors need to better understand both the insights from climate research, but also how these depend on the specific approaches, assumptions and limitations of the research they use to inform their policies, decisions and actions. These include:

- The range of uncertainties (e.g. with climate projections) and potential for climate "surprises" (linked to non-linearity of physical and economic phenomena, e.g. with climate tipping points and extreme events) associated with climate science and modelling, and though the warming of the climate system is unequivocal[15] and due to human actions.
- The implications of climate science uncertainties for a) climate mitigation (e.g. in terms of remaining carbon budget, and no agreed approach in modelling remaining carbon budgets by sector and country)[16] and b) climate adaptation and action to deal with climate impacts, including the socio-economic impacts from climate change.
- Uncertainties associated with the assumptions of climate modelling (e.g. future emissions scenarios, burden sharing in energy models). Integrated assessment models (IAMs) in particular are built to model the complex interactions between the different dimensions at the origin of climate change, seeking to enhance understanding while providing insights for policy making. A number of assumptions need to be made to model large, complex and chaotic systems and the result of this complex modelling is associated with uncertainties.

Box 7. The role of climate scenario analysis to assess climate risks, impacts and alignment

Scenario analysis is "*a process for identifying and assessing the potential implications of a range of plausible future states under conditions of uncertainty.*" Scenario analysis can be quantitative, qualitative, or a mix of both. The terms "scenario analysis", "stress test" and "sensitivity analysis" are often used interchangeably, though definitions differ.[1]

Although climate scenario analysis was recommended by the Task Force on Climate-Related Financial Disclosures (TCFD) as a tool for climate risk management for financial impact, climate scenario analysis can also be used by investors to achieve other objectives, such as climate alignment goals (i.e. to align portfolios with a climate target, as discussed previously) or to inform RBC due diligence activities.

Recognising the challenging nature of climate risks and impacts, an increasing number of industry stakeholders, central banks, financial supervisors and other stakeholders are developing climate scenarios and climate scenario analysis guidance. The IIGCC for instance has developed a framework for climate scenario analysis, which recommends establishing climate objectives (such as: aligning portfolio to a 2°C or lower future; or incorporation of climate change into selection of investments);

understanding and selecting scenarios; applying scenario analysis to investment; reviewing findings and considering actions; ongoing active monitoring; and disclosure.

Several individual asset managers and asset owners have also undertaken (or are building capacity to develop) climate scenario analysis or stress test across their portfolio or for specific sectors or geographies. They include for instance AXA Investment Managers, Sweden's pension funds (e.g. AP3), Allianz and Schroders. Several investors and insurers are also testing the alignment of their portfolios with climate goals (e.g. the 2 °C target), using various scenarios and methodologies. However, in this context, OECD research and analysis of existing financial sector alignment assessment methodologies, has found that results of such assessments are highly sensitive to the choice and practical use of climate mitigation scenarios, thereby highlighting the need for increased transparency as well as collaboration across climate science, climate policy and financial sector communities in this area.

1. A stress test is a "projection of the financial condition of a firm or economy, under a specific set of severely adverse conditions. This may be the result of several risk factors over multiple periods of time, or one risk factor that is short in duration." A sensitivity analysis is the "effect of a set of alternative assumptions regarding a future environment. A scenario used for sensitivity testing usually represents a relatively small change in these risk factors or their likelihood of occurrence."

Source: IIGCC, (2019[68]), Navigating climate scenario analysis: A guide for institutional investors, www.iigcc.org/resources/navigating-climate-scenario-analysis-a-guide-for-intuitional-investors; TCFD, (2017[69]), Technical Supplement: The Use of Scenario Analysis in Disclosure of Climate-Related Risks and Opportunities, www.tcfdhub.org/scenario-analysis; TCFD, (2017[33]), Recommendations of the Task Force on Climate-related Financial Disclosures (TCFD), Final Report, www.fsb-tcfd.org/wp-content/uploads/2017/06/FINAL-2017-TCFD-Report-11052018.pdf; TCFD, (2019[70]), Task Force on Climate-related Financial Disclosures: Status Report, www.tcfdhub.org/resource/task-force-on-climate-related-financial-disclosures-2019-status-report; UNEP FI, (2019[71]), Changing Course: A comprehensive investor guide to scenario-based methods for climate risk assessment, in response to the TCFD, www.unepfi.org/industries/investment/changing-course-a-comprehensive-investor-guide-to-scenario-based-methods-for-climate-risk-assessment-in-response-to-the-tcfd; The Shift Project for AFEP, (2019[72]), Energy and Climate Scenarios: Evaluation and guidance, theshiftproject.org/en/article/energy-climate-scenarios-evaluation-guidance-report; I4CE, (2019[73]), Understanding transition scenarios Eight steps for reading and interpreting these scenarios, www.i4ce.org/en/publication/understanding-transition-scenarios-eight-steps-for-reading-and-november-2019-interpreting-these-scenarios; NGFS, (2020[74]), NGFS Climate Scenarios for central banks and supervisors, www.ngfs.net/en/ngfs-climate-scenarios-central-banks-and-supervisors; NGFS, (2020[75]), Guide to climate scenario analysis for central banks and supervisors, www.ngfs.net/en/guide-climate-scenario-analysis-central-banks-and-supervisors; Carney, (2019[76]), Remarks given during the UN Secretary General's Climate Action Summit 2019, www.bankofengland.co.uk/speech/2019/mark-carney-remarks-at-united-nations-climate-action-summit-2019; 2° Investing Initiative, (2020[77]), PACTA 2020 Swiss Assessment: 80% of the market assessed in first-of-its kind study of the Swiss financial sector's alignment with climate goals – 2DII, 2degrees-investing.org/bridging-the-gap/, Noels and Jachnik, (2022[2]), Assessing the climate consistency of finance: taking stock of methodologies and assessing their links to climate mitigation policy objectives, www.oecd.org/environment/assessing-the-climate-consistency-of-finance-d12005e7-en.htm.

Responding to data and methodological challenges

In order to fill information gaps, lack of standardisation of metrics or outstanding methodological or modelling challenges, investors can consider engaging in individual efforts to obtain more climate-related information from investee corporations and encourage them to enhance their climate disclosure and reporting (e.g. through internal data gathering or climate surveys to investee companies), including disclosure on scope 3 emissions and other supply chain climate-relevant metrics. Investors can also participate in industry-, regulatory- and policy-led initiatives to enhance the availability of climate-related information, such as CDP (Carbon Disclosure Project). Additionally, knowledge sharing and collaboration on identifying climate impacts for example, through sector mapping in GHG emissions could be useful.

Importantly, in order to trigger engagement or action under an RBC approach, perfect information is not necessary. In this respect, most investors already have a good idea of the industries and specific companies associated with significant GHG emissions or those that are the most crucial for adaptation efforts, despite outstanding challenges with adaptation metrics and emissions pathways, as discussed subsequently. Under the *OECD Guidelines*, investors should act "as soon as possible, and in a proactive way" to avoid "serious or irreversible environmental damages resulting from their activities" and "not use the lack of full scientific certainty or pathways as a reason for postponing cost-effective measures to prevent or minimise such damage". (OECD, 2023[8])

Measure 3: Seeking to prevent and mitigate actual and potential adverse climate impacts

Under an RBC due diligence approach, investors are expected to take action in response to climate risks and impacts they have identified and prioritised with the aim of preventing or mitigating them. This measure includes: 1) influencing existing assets through engagement, active ownership and stewardship; and 2) responding to climate considerations through portfolio allocation at asset-class and asset-levels, using available investment strategies. In addition, investors may consider how their actions to seek to prevent and mitigate adverse climate impacts relate to portfolio-level considerations. The effectiveness of these actions should be tracked and measured against relevant climate objectives and targets (See Measure 4: Track implementation and results of due diligence for climate impacts) and where performance is lacking, investors may consider how approaches can be modified, intensified or rebalanced to achieve concrete results.

Influencing existing assets through engagement, active ownership and stewardship

Under the *OECD Guidelines*, investors are expected to build and exert their leverage to the extent possible to influence their underlying companies to take action to prevent and mitigate adverse climate impacts. Investors can use engagement and broader stewardship to influence investee companies to prevent and mitigate adverse climate risks and impacts. Engagement strategies are particularly important in encouraging investee companies to transition towards better climate performance.

In this respect, investors can first use their ownership stake in a company to influence its decision-making and improve their management of climate risks, impacts and opportunities, through **active engagement with investee companies to address climate impacts**. (OECD, 2022[78]) **Engagement strategies include dialogue with corporates**, **shareholder resolution and proxy voting** (NZAOA, 2022[28]); (IIGCC, 2015[79]). In particular:

- Investors can engage directly with investee corporations to encourage them to understand and take action on adverse climate impacts on society and the environment, e.g. through dialogue. Investors should set clear expectations for the actions, targets and disclosures they want to see from portfolio companies and assets on climate risks and impacts, and articulate escalation strategies and timelines if these expectations are not met.
- Investors should set clear and constructive policies for voting on climate-related resolutions, with a co-ordinated approach across the investment firm, where practical. It is important that investors publicly disclose how they have voted on climate-related resolutions, with explanations for any climate-positive resolutions they have voted against or abstained on.
- Investors should be active in setting, co-filing or supporting (including through pre-disclosure where permitted) resolutions that are consistent with their climate policies and with the goal of aligning with the Paris Agreement, including on topics such as credible emission-reduction targets and fossil-fuel phase-out.
- Where relevant, investors can engage with investee corporations and associated project developers to ensure that they undertake *ex ante* and *ex post* environmental and social impact assessment (ESIA) that consider climate risks and impacts and develop strategies on climate mitigation and adaptation, e.g. for infrastructure or real estate projects, but also other assets (Equator Principles, 2023[80]). ESIA are typically part of the process required of infrastructure

projects to secure government permits to implement new investments or expand existing operations.

- Investors can also engage directly with investee companies to encourage and help them build adaptive capacity to climate impacts. For instance, investors can work with the developer or manager of new or existing assets to improve their resilience (through e.g. upgraded engineering requirements).
- Despite leverage limitations to engage across specific asset classes, such as fixed income, there are opportunities for investors to engage both as shareholders and bondholders, as discussed further (see section on Availability and feasibility of investment strategies and leverage limitations).
- Beyond bilateral engagement, investors can also take action to tackle climate impacts or achieve climate goals through **advocacy, multi-stakeholder action or industry initiatives**. Shareholders can make use of their shareholder rights to hold boards accountable regarding climate change and other RBC issues. Shareholder rights include notably proxy statements, shareholder voting and transparent mechanisms for electing and holding boards accountable. In this respect, several international initiatives aim to foster engagement from institutional investors and investee corporations in support of climate goals. For example, as part of the Climate Action 100+ initiative, (Climate Action 100+, 2023[81]), asset managers encourage corporations to better manage climate risks. Other examples of coalitions or initiatives include the Glasgow Financial Alliance for Net-Zero (GFANZ), (which is the umbrella organisation for other coalitions such as the NZAOA, the Net-Zero Asset Manager Initiative and the Net-Zero Insurance Alliance) or the IIGCC's Paris Aligned Investment Initiative.

Investors who engage with investee companies or asset owners who engage with asset managers on climate impacts and risks may wish to adopt **engagement targets** in order to track activities and progress with individual corporates and asset managers. For instance, at the time of writing, the NZAOA requires its members to engage, at a minimum, 20 companies in their portfolio, with a focus on companies responsible for the most "owned emissions" or on companies responsible for a combined 65% of "owned emissions" in their portfolio (NZAOA, 2022[28]).

Taking climate considerations into account in portfolio allocation at asset-class or asset-level

Within the limits of their various mandates, investors can also use investment strategies, which recognise the implications of climate impact and direct capital away from companies with poor climate practices. (OECD, 2017[7]) Various investment strategies are available for investors to take climate considerations (including adverse impacts, risks and opportunities) into account, whether at asset- or asset-class level. Such strategies can help investors by I) reducing portfolios exposure to emissions intensive assets or assets not compatible with climate resilience; or (ii) increasing exposure to low-carbon, resilient assets.

Potentially relevant investment strategies are outlined below with the understanding that strategies will vary across investors based on their mandates, legal and operational contexts. It is also important to note that investment strategies which are limited to managing financially material climate risks may not be sufficient to address climate risks and impacts under an RBC due diligence approach. Investment strategies that are purely driven by traditional risk management considerations may lead to investment and divestment decisions that can run counter to overall societal considerations regarding engagement and access to transition finance in high-emitting sectors or regarding access to adaptation finance for sectors and geographies exposed to higher resilience risks. As such, exposure to climate risk and impacts, as well as broader considerations related to accelerating the transition through engagement as opposed to disengagement, should be considered alongside standard risk and return objectives when making investment decisions to the extent this aligns with an investor's mandate and fiduciary duties (OECD, 2017[3]).

Relevant investment strategies under an RBC due diligence approach include:

- **Best-in-class:** Investors can use best-in-class investing strategies (positive screening) to drive investment towards the best-performing companies within each sector or industry, according to climate factors, such as carbon footprint or climate resilience.
- **ESG Tilting Strategies focused on climate**: Investors can raise the threshold for inclusion of key carbon-intensive sectors according to GHG emissions levels, using ESG tilting strategies. However, OECD research suggests that ESG and climate scoring methodologies may not necessarily be suitable on their own for investors seeking to better align their portfolios with low-carbon economies, due to lack of integrity of methodologies and metrics (Boffo et al., 2020[57]; Noels and Jachnik, 2022[2]) and may need to be accompanied by additional checks by investors to avoid the risk of greenwashing (See above). Additional efforts are needed to improve market integrity, clarity and transparency and address greenwashing issues, especially for ESG tilting and other ESG investing strategies in listed and index investing, whether under passive or active investing mandates.
- **Divestment:**
    - For active strategies, **investors can choose to reduce the investment position in light of the climate risks identified,** where appropriate, and communicate the reason for the reduction to the investee corporation. Investors may consider this action if engagement actions have failed (see previous section on engagement and stewardship). Alternative actions for active investing include temporary divestment (while pursuing ongoing climate risk mitigation as appropriate and where possible); or full divestment (e.g. after failed attempts at mitigation). Divestment can be applied across several asset classes, though it is typically most applicable to listed equities and fixed income (NZAOA, 2022[28]).
    - For passive strategies, where possible and in compliance with regulatory obligations, **investors may redesign their passive investment strategy** to avoid investing in assets related to significant climate impacts (e.g. exiting a passive index and investing in an adjusted or tailored index or benchmark, or excluding assets associated with significant actual or potential climate impacts identified by the investor).
    - It is worth noting that under the *OECD Guidelines*, divestment should in most cases be a last resort or reserved only for the most severe adverse impacts (OECD, 2017[7]). In addition, divesting from assets associated with adverse climate impacts may limit the adverse climate impacts of investors' portfolios without reducing the overall impact on society and the environment, due to purchase of the asset by another investor, or may in fact slow needed transition in high-emitting assets and sectors. There is an important difference between reducing emissions in an investment portfolio and reducing emissions in the real economy (NZAOA, 2022[28]). Divesting can also be associated with considerations regarding a just transition, for example in relation to impacts on employment and development. However, divesting from assets within, but not across, a sector can send important market signals and enhance the competitive position of best-in-class actors in the sector.
- **Exclusion or negative screening:** For both active and passive strategies, investors can screen potential investments to exclude companies with significant climate risk and impact, based on their carbon-intensity (e.g. coal) or other metrics or criteria in exclusionary policies. In some cases, exclusion may be a first response to adverse climate impacts. For example, some investment institutions have exclusion policies for highly damaging industries or products or those with potential systemic negative impacts (OECD, 2017[7]).

Additionally, investors can contribute to climate objectives and sustainable development more broadly through orienting investments towards assets aligned with low-carbon, climate-resilient pathways.

- **Thematic investment:** Thematic investment can enable investors to increase portfolios' exposure to assets aligned with low-carbon, climate-resilient pathways. This can be done whether through investment in thematic funds or direct investment in low-carbon, resilient assets. Thematic investment portfolios dedicated to addressing adverse climate impacts and risks can include (See also Box 8 and Box 9):
  - Fixed-income assets (e.g. corporate or project-level green bonds, or green bond indices or funds).[17] It is important to note that green bonds and other green financial products face similar risk of greenwashing as ESG index investing. For example, although green bonds continue to be a focal point for green finance, a 2020 study by the Bank for International Settlements indicates that "green bond projects have not necessarily translated into comparatively low or falling carbon emissions at the firm level." (Ehlers, 2020[82]). Therefore, as with the use of third-party ESG ratings, investors should apply their own climate due diligence processes to assess whether a green bond is consistent with their climate policies, rather than solely relying on the "green" label.
  - Direct or co-investment in brownfield and greenfield low-carbon, resilient infrastructure and real estate (e.g. energy efficiency or renewable power).
  - Private equity or private debt in companies with activities that directly contribute to mitigating or adapting to climate change (e.g. manufacturers of solar panels, wind turbines or electric vehicles).
  - Listed equity or debt, e.g. through investing in climate-friendly benchmarks for index investing, as part of thematic investing, or broader integration of climate factors in index investing strategies (such as the EU Climate Transition and Paris Aligned Benchmarks).

For investors who have adopted climate change mitigation targets and objectives under an RBC due diligence approach, or under a climate alignment approach, successfully delivering climate change mitigation goals requires a plurality of decarbonisation approaches. Beyond economic activities that are demonstrably low-carbon (e.g. renewable power), most economic activities today do not qualify yet as low-carbon, low-emissions or net-zero emissions. Transforming economies with differing structures to lower- and net-zero-carbon is an unprecedented challenge. As a result, investors should consider approaches to enable a progressive shift towards lower emissions throughout the economy, through low carbon "transition finance" (OECD, 2022[19]). To identify the core features of transition finance, the OECD hast reviewed the transition relevant taxonomies, guidance and principles by selected public and private actors, as well as various transition relevant financial instruments and produced work on emerging approaches and instruments to highlight commonalities, divergences as well as issues to consider for coherent market development and progress towards global environmental objectives (Tandon, 2021[62]).

Box 8. Institutional investment in green infrastructure opportunities

Direct or co-investment in low-carbon, resilient infrastructure projects can help to mitigate adverse climate impacts. Although it can generate higher margins than other strategies, direct investment in infrastructure can be costly as it requires institutional investors to build internal capacity and new investment teams with expertise in green investments. Investors may also face other challenges such as lack of sufficient market depth in the absence of pipelines of bankable projects with sufficient risk-adjusted return; or regulatory constraints or disincentives (e.g. linked to prudential regulations). As a result, investment in green infrastructure still accounts for only a small fraction of institutional portfolios.

Institutional investors wishing to increase direct investment in low-carbon, climate-resilient assets will typically need to address capacity gaps, by developing in-house expertise. This may involve hiring or training new investment teams with technical or investment expertise in low-carbon, resilient assets.

Investors, with support from policy makers, should share success stories associated with climate-friendly investment opportunities to increase awareness. Securitised products related to green infrastructure can also be developed for investors with a preference for liquidity. Financial instruments by public financial institutions can also help mobilise and catalyse institutional investors' participation in green infrastructure, such as risk alleviators (e.g. loans, co-investments and cornerstone stakes) and transaction enablers (e.g. warehousing and pooling). Investors can also collaborate with governments and other public and private stakeholders to create a pipeline of bankable projects, including in green infrastructure as an asset class.

Sources: OECD, (2020[36]), Green Infrastructure in the Decade for Delivery: Assessing Institutional Investment, doi.org/10.1787/24090344; Röttgers et al., (2018[83]), OECD Progress Update on Approaches to Mobilising Institutional Investment for Sustainable Infrastructure: Background paper to the G20 Sustainable Finance Study Group – Environment Working Paper No. 138, dx.doi.org/10.1787/45426991-en; OECD, (2013[35]), High-level principles of long-term investment financing by institutional investors, www.oecd.org/finance/private-pensions/G20-OECD-Principles-LTI-Financing.pdf; CDP, (2019[84]), Major risk or rosy opportunity – Are companies ready for climate change?, www.cdp.net/en/research/global-reports/global-climate-change-report-2018/climate-report-risks-and-opportunities; Global Commission on Adaptation, (2019[85]), Adapt Now: A Global Call for Leadership on Climate Resilience, gca.org/reports/adapt-now-a-global-call-for-leadership-on-climate-resilience.

Box 9. Thematic investment towards adaptation

Thematic investment to increase the share of low-carbon assets will mostly be in low-carbon infrastructure (Box 8), in addition to sustainable land-use. Thematic investment can also take the form of allocating capital towards adaptation. Investors can for example invest in assets and instruments that help anticipate, absorb, accommodate or recover from the risks and impacts of physical climate risks or help build resilience. This can involve:

- Investment in **adaptation investments that "climate proof" infrastructure**, reducing the exposure or vulnerability of an infrastructure asset or network, whether from the outset or as part of a retrofitting process (e.g. building to higher design standards, considering reduced exposure when siting or designing or pursuing a different approach to provide the same service).
- Investing in **nature-based solutions (or NbS)** which are measures that protect, sustainably manage, or restore nature, with the goal of maintaining or enhancing ecosystem services to address a variety of social, environmental and economic challenges (OECD, 2020[86]). NbS are recognised as key to effectively adapting to adverse climate impacts. Examples of NbS investments that climate proof infrastructure include increasing green spaces in cities to reduce storm water runoff during heavy rain events, through increased absorption, or investments in mangrove forests, which decrease wave energy and storm surges and thereby reduce the need for coastal protection infrastructure.

Responding to climate considerations at portfolio level

Responding to adverse climate impacts, risks and opportunities at portfolio level can inform all different types of investment strategies adopted by investors across and within asset classes. Assets can be allocated across different investment opportunities, so as to achieve long-term objectives of the investors (IIGCC, 2020[24]). In particular:

- Investors can adjust their strategy or other similar process by defining an optimal portfolio allocation in line with the climate objectives and targets they may have adopted (see Measure 1: Embed climate considerations into policies and management systems and Measure 4: Track implementation and results of due diligence for climate impacts), and along standard risk and return objectives and other constraints.

- Investors can also clarify how to implement asset allocation, e.g. by changing investment mandates or benchmarks (IIGCC, 2020[24]).
- To identify the most appropriate opportunities given their existing constraints, investors can undertake a cross-section analysis of the climate-related investment opportunities by asset classes, and map those against climate related asset allocation targets in place (IIGCC, 2015[79]).
- Investors also need to ensure consistency and alignment of allocation decisions with adopted climate objectives and targets over time as part of their RBC due diligence approach (see Measure 4: Track implementation and results of due diligence for climate impacts

Availability and feasibility of investment strategies and leverage limitations

The decision of an investor to adopt a given investment strategy will depend upon corporate governance rules as well as institutional investors' investment policy, mandate and implementation across portfolio management strategies (e.g. passive or active investing); asset classes and investment types (e.g. listed equity, fixed income, private equity, infrastructure, etc.); and fund sizes. Those factors may hinder the investor's ability to influence a company by using its leverage to mitigate the adverse climate impact or risk identified. For instance:

- Passive investment managers may require client consent to exclude a company from an index. In addition, for passive index investing, adopting best-in-class investing, ESG screening tailored to climate change, or exclusionary screening, requires tilting index strategies to incorporate climate factors.
- Available investment strategies depend on the characteristic of an asset class. Active ownership and engagement for instance is less relevant for fixed income, though engagement remains available for bondholders, e.g. in the due diligence process before purchase (NZAOA, 2022[28]).
- Corporate governance rules may impede minority shareholders, especially foreign shareholders, from exercising influence over publicly traded companies.

Though there are practical limitations on the ability of investors to effect change in the behaviour of investee companies, under the *OECD Guidelines*, the degree of leverage of an investor over the company causing the adverse (climate) impact is useful in considering what it can do to persuade that entity to take action, but not when considering whether the investor should carry out due diligence and effectively exercise any leverage it may have (OECD, 2017[7]). For example, in the context of private equity, LPs may be able to work with the GP that hold a majority shareholding in private equity, infrastructure and real estate funds to influence investee companies.

Measure 4: Track implementation and results of due diligence for climate impacts

In order to ensure RBC due diligence activities are impactful and effective, it is important that investors both track their own performance against their policies (including objectives and targets related to climate), as well as monitor investee companies' efforts in preventing and mitigating climate impacts. Such tracking involves 1) developing objectives, targets and identifying benchmarks to track climate performance at a portfolio and asset level and 2) tracking actual performance against those targets and benchmarks.

Developing objectives, targets and benchmarks to track climate performance at portfolio, asset-class and asset level

It is important that investors monitor and track implementation and effectiveness of the enterprise's own internal commitments. This may involve tracking against climate objectives and targets (e.g. to align their portfolios with Paris Agreement goals) at asset-class and portfolio level. (IIGCC, 2020[24]; NZAOA, 2022[28]). It may also involve tracking the implementation and effectiveness of activities and goals on due diligence. Establishing appropriate quantitative and qualitative indicators is important to tracking. This may involve:

- Setting objectives and indicators related to engagement with investee companies associated with significant climate risks or promoting green and just transition.
- Setting objectives and indicators with respect to support of green infrastructure or nature-based solutions.
- Setting absolute emissions reduction and climate adaptation targets at portfolio level to inform asset allocation[18] and monitoring impact of strategy (e.g. by setting targets for total absolute emissions reductions and emissions intensity reductions. Benchmarking strategies to a steady-state portfolio can allow for emissions trends resulting from the investee companies and assets to be distinguished from the effect of changes in portfolio composition.
- Setting targets and goals within each asset class (e.g. sovereign bonds, real estate, private equity, listed equity and corporate fixed income including from financial institution borrowers).
- Setting interim targets, e.g. medium-term targets to 2035 and short-term targets to 2025. These targets should be ambitious and reflect the urgent need for a downward inflection in emissions, with appropriate buffers built-in to accommodate the uncertainties in the IPCC modelling.
- Defining actions to be taken if targets are missed or if the portfolio is not on track to meet those targets (on an interpolated basis in the interim years between target dates).

Both the NZAOA and the IIGCC PAII have developed suggested portfolio and asset class targets for investors who wish to align their portfolios with net zero emissions pathways (NZAOA, 2022[28]); (IIGCC, 2020[24]). The Science Based Targets initiative (SBTi) has also developed a methodology to help companies and investors set short- and medium-term emissions reduction targets that are consistent with a Paris-aligned pathway, and it has developed a global standard for net-zero business, including through a validation protocol (SBTi, 2021[29])

Investor associations and civil society can also support investors in defining appropriate objectives, targets and developing benchmarks that reflect the investors' and investee corporations' progress in meeting those targets. Policymakers also have an important role to play in improving market and environmental integrity of benchmarks and encouraging harmonisation, comparability and consistency of benchmarks. In this respect, an increasing number of benchmarks are being developed to help investors identify corporates' climate performance. Investors who have adopted climate goals (e.g. net zero goals) can use benchmarks and indices that reflect investee companies' performance against a set of climate criteria (e.g. in terms of climate alignment and transition), and by weighting investee companies in benchmarks. (IIGCC, 2021[37]). In the context of project and asset finance transactions, and thus more applicable to international banking institutions, the Equator Principles has also published guidance on how investors can address climate risks and impacts, both from a financial materiality and environmental integrity perspectives, from projects, assets and infrastructure they finance. (Equator Principles, 2023[80])

Box 10. Challenges with developing granular pathways

Available emissions pathways developed by climate modellers and policy makers typically remain at a relatively high level of geographical and sectoral aggregation. As a result, they may not necessarily provide the level of granularity needed for investors to define the emissions reduction and investment trajectories available or needed across their portfolio, asset classes and investment mandates.

Investors may therefore face challenges to identifying global, regional and sectoral pathways needed to meet the climate objectives or targets adopted as part of an RBC due diligence approach. Pathways refer to modelled emissions, technology and investment trajectories needed to achieve a given climate goal or objective. While global pathways are available which can be used for portfolio analysis, investors face gaps to identify and develop robust pathways and investment trajectories broken down by sector and region relevant for analyses at the level of individual assets and asset classes. An increasing number of initiatives review available pathways for investors. GFANZ for instance has developed guidance to help financial institutions in understanding and comparing sectoral pathways, facilitate engagement between financial institutions and their clients and portfolio firms, and communicate pathway needs to developers.

Multi-strategy investors typically need to look at their exposures to different sectors and regions across asset classes and aggregate these trajectories to understand overall pathways to respond to climate risks. Such pathways and related targets will also depend on investors' preferences for managing climate risks at the portfolio, asset class- or asset-levels, across key sectors and geographies, as discussed under Measure 3: Seeking to prevent and mitigate actual and potential adverse climate impacts.

Sources: IIGCC, (2020[24]), Net Zero Investment Framework for Consultation, www.iigcc.org; IIGCC, (2021[37]), Net Zero Investment Framework 1.5 C - Implementation Guide, www.parisalignedinvestment.org/media/2021/03/PAII-Net-Zero-Investment-Framework_Implementation-Guide.pdf; GFANZ, (2022[87]), Guidance on use of Sectoral pathways for financial institutions, assets.bbhub.io/company/sites/63/2021/11/GFANZ-Progress-Report.pdf; NZAOA, (2022[28]),. UN-convened Net-Zero Asset Owner Alliance Target Setting Protocol, www.unepfi.org/net-zero-alliance/resources/target-setting-protocol-second-edition.

Tracking GHG performance against benchmarks and targets

Investors can use various metrics to track climate performance on a portfolio level and across asset classes. As discussed above, performance against climate objectives and targets, as well as adequate reporting against such targets will be an important indicator of effectiveness of due diligence.

Metrics related to measuring climate mitigation often are based on the climate footprint or exposure at a portfolio level (TCFD, 2017[33]). These include:

- **Carbon footprint**, or **total carbon emissions**, which measures the absolute GHG emissions associated with a portfolio, expressed in tons CO2e.
- **Carbon intensity**, a metric for identifying portfolio areas with exposure to carbon-intensive assets or exposure to low-carbon technologies. It can be used to measure and compare carbon emissions across a portfolio normalised by the market value of the portfolio, expressed in tons CO2e / USD Million invested. **Weighted average carbon intensity** is also used, which measures a portfolio's exposure to carbon-intensive companies, expressed in tons CO2e / USD Million revenue. The TCFD recommends asset owners and asset managers to use this metric to report to their beneficiaries and clients.

- **Exposure to carbon-related assets,**[19] which measures the amount or percentage of carbon-related assets in the portfolio, expressed in USD million or percentage of the current portfolio value.

Exposure or footprinting metrics have important limitations, since they are often limited to scope 1 and scope 2 emissions, while the most relevant scope 3 emissions are often challenging to account for. Unless combined with alignment targets and tracked over time, they may fail to provide forward-looking information on a portfolios' alignments with relevant transition pathways. As target-setting by companies increases (in frequency and quality), investors can benefit from incorporating forward-looking metrics into their portfolio tracking, with analysis on the delivery against targets by portfolio companies over time.

To address these limitations, using different complementary methodologies and indicators that cover and assess decarbonisation progress can prove useful. Over time, indicators on the actual performance against corporate targets will become more essential to evaluate actual progress. In order to provide a more nuanced perspective, to include credibility considerations, and to link more closely to real-economy actions, there is also a need to look beyond GHG emission-based metrics only, e.g. by also analysing forward looking capacity, production and capital expenditure plans of companies (Noels and Jachnik, 2022[2]).

As further highlighted by OECD studies (Noels and Jachnik, 2022[2]), as a pre-condition for being able to produce portfolio-level metrics, methodologies and metrics related to measuring the climate footprint or exposure need to be developed and applied at the level of specific assets or asset classes. Additionally, asset-relevant metrics may be complemented by:

- Other types **of emission intensity** or **carbon intensity** metrics. Such performance metrics express emissions from a given product, economic activity per a relevant unit of measure and may be useful in identifying best-in-class performers and conversely also assets and investees with scope for improvement. Emission intensity metrics usefully are meant to reflect a full life cycle analysis (EU TEG, 2020[59]).
- Metrics related to **capital expenditures, revenues, costs, assets, and liabilities**.
- Metrics and complementary indicators related to **progress such as measures of the presence and characteristics of concrete transition plans** (including to upscale climate solutions), which can further help put GHG-based alignment assessment results in perspective and provide a more holistic view.

It is important that metrics are transparent with regard to their basis and methodology (scenarios, thresholds, targets) and in turn their alignment with overall climate targets or objectives (also see Box 11). In this respect, the *OECD Guidelines* also provide that "[i]t will be important to report against, review and update targets regularly in relation to their adequacy and relevance, based on the latest available scientific evidence and as different national or industry specific transition pathways are developed and updated." (OECD, 2023[8])

While many metrics exist to measure progress with respect to climate mitigation; resilience and adaptation indicators are typically more diffuse and complex (Leiter and Olhoff, 2019[56]). In this respect, additional work is necessary to establish comprehensive and useful metrics for adaptation across economic activities and underlying assets.

Importantly, the results of tracking should inform other aspects of the due diligence processes. For example, where targets are not being met approaches to prevention and mitigation may need to be modified (see Measure 3: Seeking to prevent and mitigate actual and potential adverse climate impacts).

Box 11. Assessing the alignment of investments and financing with climate policy objectives: definitions, data, methodologies and their applications

Article 2.1c of the Paris Agreement calls for "Making finance flows consistent with a pathway towards low greenhouse gas emissions and climate-resilient development". In this context, the OECD conducts work to explore data, methods and approaches for policy makers and financial sector stakeholders to assess the degree of alignment or misalignment of investments and financing with respect to national or international climate objectives and targets.

Over 2019-21, three initial country-sector level pilot studies for the manufacturing industries in Norway, the transport sector in Latvia, and the buildings sector in the United Kingdom, with a focus on investments in real economy assets, which directly lock-in or help reduce GHG emissions. From the perspective of national accounts, this corresponds to assessing the climate alignment of Gross Fixed Capital Formation (GFCF). The pilot studies tested a range of "reference points" and benchmarks, such as international and national scenarios or trajectories, taxonomies, performance thresholds or other types of quantified and time-bound targets. Findings highlight that real economy investments are only very partially aligned, but that different reference points lead to varying results. Further, such studies show limitations in sourcing granular data (on targets and pathways, GHG performance of assets, as well as investments and financing sources) from multiple sources with varying quality, granularity, and coverage.

While the availability of such data may currently be limited in some areas, improvements are underway. As an increasing number of economic actors are defining Paris Alignment strategies and targets, the disclosure of climate-related financial and non-financial data is being mandated or incentivised. In this context, further analysis assessed methodologies and metrics for tracking the alignment of financial assets with the Paris Agreement's mitigation provision. Such work finds that a range of different and complex methodological choices, as well as current scope and data limitations, impact the environmental integrity and policy relevance of alignment or misalignment results. Suggestions for improved and more comprehensive financial sector alignment assessment. These include the development of different complementary methodologies to cover a broader range of financial asset classes than the current main focus on listed corporate equity, the development of more tailored mitigation scenarios by climate policy and science communities, better communication of uncertainties by all stakeholders, and the need for a series of indicators to assess progress and impacts that include but are not limited to GHG-based alignment assessments.

Source: OECD, (2021[88]), Research Collaborative on Tracking Finance for Climate Action, www.oecd.org/env/researchcollaborative; UNFCCC, (2015[1]), The Paris Agreement, unfccc.int/process-and-meetings/the-paris-agreement; Dobrinevski and Jachnik, (2020[89]), Exploring options to measure the climate consistency of real economy investments: The manufacturing industries of Norway, doi.org/10.1787/1012bd81-en; Dobrinevski and Jachnik, (2020[90]), Exploring options to measure the climate consistency of real economy investments: The transport sector in Latvia, doi.org/10.1787/48d53aac-en; Dobrinevski and Jachnik, (2021[91]), Measuring the alignment of real economy investments with climate mitigation objectives: The United Kingdom's buildings sector, doi.org/10.1787/82cc3a4c-en; Jachnik, Mirabile and Dobrinevski, (2019[92]), Tracking finance flows towards assessing their consistency with climate objectives, doi.org/10.1787/82cc3a4c-en; Noels and Jachnik, (2022[2]), Assessing the climate consistency of finance: taking stock of methodologies and assessing their links to climate mitigation policy objectives, doi.org/10.1787/d12005e7-en.

Measure 5: Communicate how climate risks and impacts are addressed

Communication is a key aspect of the RBC due diligence process as it allows investors to demonstrate due diligence with respect to climate impacts and allows market participants, regulators, and other stakeholders to understand the level of ambition and effectiveness of an investor's due diligence process. This measure involves 1) publicly reporting relevant information on due diligence processes and their outcomes and 2) as relevant, communicating with stakeholders as to how climate risks and impacts are addressed.

Publicly reporting relevant information on due diligence processes and their outcomes

Under the RBC due diligence process, investors are encouraged to report on how climate issues have been integrated into policy and risk management, areas of significant risk and impacts and importantly, how risks and impacts are being addressed as well as performance against benchmarks and targets over time. This allows for disclosures which reflect not only current climate impacts but also the investors' performance and progress over time in addressing climate issues. Specifically, investors are encouraged to report on: (OECD, 2017[7]); (OECD, 2018[5]):

- The investor climate policy.
- Information on measures taken to embed climate considerations into policies and management systems.
- The investor's identified areas of significant climate risks and impacts, the significant adverse climate impacts and risks identified, prioritised and assessed, as well as the prioritisation criteria.
- The actions taken to prevent or mitigate those risks, including as relevant: investment strategies considered or adopted across asset classes, engagement activities undertaken by the investor; companies with which the investor has engaged; results of engagement with specific companies; decisions regarding divestment; voting records of investor in investee company shareholder meetings and guidelines for voting in investee companies.
- Investor's climate plans, metrics and targets, and where possible estimated timelines and benchmarks for improvement; measures to track implementation and results; and outcomes in term of progress against plans and targets.
- As relevant the provision of or co-operation in any remediation of climate impacts.

In recent years, various reporting and disclosure schemes, whether international or domestic, mandatory and voluntary, have been introduced calling for and providing guidance on climate related disclosures. In some geographies this has included reporting expectations related to RBC due diligence.[20] Leading reporting frameworks include disclosure expectations that cover many of the same areas called for under due diligence reporting, although from varying materiality perspectives (see Table 1). This mapping indicates that reporting expectations under the OECD due diligence framework can largely be met through using existing reporting frameworks provided they also consider climate risks and impacts from an environmental and social impact perspective. It may also require reporting additional information not covered in current frameworks. See Table 1 on Due diligence reporting expectations compared to leading disclosure frameworks.

Table 1. Due diligence reporting expectations compared to leading disclosure frameworks.

Public disclosure expectations under OECD RBC due diligence framework	TCFD	CDP	CDSB	GRI	SASB
Investor climate policy, including due diligence approaches	Not explicitly mentioned.	Not explicitly mentioned.	Not explicitly mentioned.	Approach to due diligence.	Not explicitly mentioned.
Information on measures taken to embed climate issues into policies and management systems, and across asset classes.	Governance processes with respect to climate risks and opportunities (* from a financial materiality perspective).	Board's oversight of climate-related issues. Management-level positions with responsibility for climate-related issues.	Governance of environmental policies, strategy and information.	Governance structure, strategy and profile of the organisation for climate issues. Committees or executive-level positions responsible for decision-making on environmental topics.	Aligned with TCFD recommendations
Investors' identified areas of significant climate risks and impacts, the significant adverse climate impacts and risks identified, prioritised and assessed.	Process for identification, assessment and management of climate-related risks, including prioritisation criteria. Scope1-3 emissions and related-GHG risks and metrics used. Climate-related risks and opportunities where such information is material and relevant to the business strategy (i.e. from a financial materiality perspective)	Process for – identifying and assessing climate risks and opportunities. Whether portfolio's risk exposure is assessed and how. Details of risks and opportunities identified with the potential to have substantive financial or strategic impact on business activities. (i.e. from a financial materiality perspective). Gross global combined scope 1 and scope 2 emissions for the reporting year in metric tons CO2e per unit currency total revenue. Sales of GHG products.	The material current and anticipated environmental risks and opportunities affecting the organisation. (i.e. from a financial materiality perspective). Sources of environmental impact: GHG emissions, resource use, type of energy consumption, waste etc. Absolute and normalised scope 1 and 2 GHG emissions In CO2e metric tonnes.	Process for identifying, assessing, and prioritising climate risks and opportunities. Risks/opportunitie s posed by climate change with the potential to impact operations, revenue, or expenditure. (i.e. from a financial materiality perspective). Scope 1, 2 and 3 GHG emissions, GHG emissions intensity, Emissions ODS, NOx, Sox and other significant air emissions.	Process for identifying, assessing and prioritising climate risks and opportunities. Risk assessment and management at 3 levels: specific, systematic and systemic risks. (i.e. from a financial materiality perspective). Sources of environmental impact. Scope 1, 2, and 3 GHG emissions across all industries.
The actions taken to prevent or mitigate those risks including relevant investment strategies considered or adopted across asset classes, engagement activities undertaken by the investor etc. Investors' future climate plans, metrics and targets, and.	Targets used to manage climate risks and performance against such targets.	Processes for responding to climate risks and opportunities. Process of verification and monitoring of results Absolute emissions targets, emission intensity	Management's environmental policies and targets, including the indicators, plans and timelines to assess performance. To what extent identified risks are	Targets, performance against targets and lessons learned. Timeline for managing risks. GHG emissions reduced as a direct result of reduction	Targets, performance against targets and lessons learned.

Where possible estimated timelines and benchmarks for improvement and their outcomes Measures to track implementation and results.		targets, methane reduction targets and other emission reduction initiatives.	mitigated, and opportunities are maximised and how.	initiatives, in metric tons of CO2 equivalent.	
	Not explicitly mentioned: Specific actions taken to prevent or mitigate climate risks including relevant investment strategies considered or adopted across asset classes, engagement activities undertaken by the investor etc.	Not explicitly mentioned: Specific actions taken to prevent or mitigate climate risks including relevant strategies investment strategies considered or adopted across asset classes, engagement activities undertaken by the investor etc. Estimated timelines and benchmarks for improvement and their outcomes.	Not explicitly mentioned: Monitoring and tracking processes	Not explicitly mentioned: Particular emission reduction initiatives. Specific actions taken to prevent or mitigate climate risks including relevant strategies investment strategies considered or adopted across asset classes, engagement activities undertaken by the investor etc.	Not explicitly mentioned: Specific actions taken to prevent or mitigate climate risks including relevant strategies investment strategies considered or adopted across asset classes, engagement activities undertaken by the investor etc.

Communication to other stakeholders

In addition to public reporting, investors can also communicate internally and externally to stakeholders (including staff, beneficiaries' and other interested parties such as civil society and local communities) on their climate policy, and adverse impacts and risks related to investee companies and assets. Engaging with civil society and local communities can also help investors understand the relationship between climate and other environmental and social human rights issues, as well as the potential trade-offs between the desired climate outcomes and the desired social outcomes.

Measure 6: Encourage investees to provide for or co-operate in remediation when appropriate

Under the *OECD Guidelines*, when an enterprise contributes to an adverse impact, it should provide for or co-operate in remediation. Where an investee company is assessed as contributing to climate change impacts, the investor should apply efforts to encourage the investee company to provide for or co-operate in remediation.

As climate impacts are collective, transboundary and diffuse, the extent to which an investee company or asset can be considered to be contributing to climate impacts is complex.

The *OECD Guidelines* provide that where it is not possible to assess the extent of an enterprise's contribution to an adverse environmental impact based on available science and information, such assessment should consider "*the extent to which its activities are consistent with widely recognised standards, environmental management processes and safeguards regarding good environmental practice;*

benchmarks and standards established in applicable environmental rules and regulatory frameworks; and relevant international agreements." (OECD, 2023[8])

Where an investee company is assessed to be contributing to climate impacts, investors should encourage them to provide for or co-operation in remediation. Remediation can involve a variety of actions including restoration and taking measures to prevent future climate impacts for example through adopting cleaner technologies or making changes to business models and activities.

Box 12. Trends in climate litigation and attribution science

Climate-related litigation is increasing worldwide. Climate cases against companies and governments have nearly doubled over the last three years. Typically, climate-related claims fall under the following categories: (i) failure to mitigate GHG emissions; (ii) failure to adapt to climate physical impacts; (iii) failure to adapt investment strategies; (iv) failure to disclose climate risks; (v) failure to comply with environmental and other regulatory obligations; (vi) failure to adapt professional services or advice; (vii) failure of fiduciaries related to the above categories of claims. In several jurisdictions for instance, plaintiffs have made claims against companies or investment funds for failing to incorporate climate risk into investment decisions, and for failing to disclose climate risk to their beneficiaries.

Climate litigation often faces challenges with establishing a causal link between a particular source or group of sources of GHG emissions, and specific climate-related adverse impacts. Attribution science studies the relationship between climate change and weather events and impacts, i.e. the extent to which a particular event is attributable to anthropogenic climate change. It remains difficult to attribute specific climate-related adverse impacts to a particular source or group of sources of GHG emissions (Setzer and Byrnes, 2019[93]). Ongoing progress in attribution science is likely to change the legal landscape. In particular, it may increase liability risk for investors, corporations and even governments (e.g. for failure to adapt to climate change, or to prepare for extreme weather events). Courts might notably consider the idea of individual corporate or investor responsibility for adverse climate impact or harm, if attribution science can prove contributory or partial causation with respect to the conduct of the defendant (Marjanac et al., 2017[94]).

Sources: UNEP, (2021[95]), Global Climate Litigation Report: 2020 Status Review, www.unep.org/resources/report/global-climate-litigation-report-2020-status-review; Setzer and Byrnes, (2019[93]), Global trends in climate change litigation: 2019 snapshot, www.lse.ac.uk/granthaminstitute/publication/global-trends-in-climate-change-litigation-2020-snapshot; Sabin Center for Climate Change Law, (2020[96]), US Climate Change Litigation, climatecasechart.com/us-climate-change-litigation; Clyde & Co, (2019[97]), Climate change: Liability risks for businesses, directors and officers, online.flippingbook.com/view/648937/2; Clyde & Co, (2018[98]), The rising tide of climate change liability, resilience.clydeco.com/articles/the-rising-tide-of-climate-change-liability; Chiara, (2018[99]), Corporate Responsibility for Climate Change: Litigation and Other Grievance Mechanisms, www.asser.nl/DoingBusinessRight/Blog/post/corporate-responsibility-for-climate-change-litigation-and-other-grievance-mechanisms-by-elisa-chiaro; UNEP, (2016[100]), Lenders and Investors Environmental Liability: How Much is Too Much?, wedocs.unep.org/20.500.11822/7521; Marjanac et al., (2017[94]), Acts of god, human influence and litigation, doi.org/10.1038/ngeo3019; Ang, (2020[101]),

Investors can also encourage investee companies to participate in dialogue or remediation processes regarding climate impacts where issues are raised by stakeholders or other actors.

Legitimate remediation mechanisms can also include State-based or non-State-based processes through which grievances concerning enterprise-related adverse impacts can be raised and remedy can be sought. These include:

- Legal processes such as prosecution, litigation and arbitration.
- Non-judicial state-based mechanisms such as specialist government bodies, consumer protection agencies, regulatory oversight bodies, environmental protection agencies. The National Contact

Points to the *OECD Guidelines* are a State-based non-judicial mechanism through which issues can be raised about implementation of the *OECD Guidelines* in specific instances (See Box 13).

- Operational-level grievance mechanisms where they meet the core criteria of legitimacy, accessibility, predictability, equitability, compatibility with the *OECD Guidelines*, transparency and being dialogue-based.
- Non-state processes such as Global Framework Agreements between companies and Global Trade Unions, multi-stakeholder grievance mechanisms, community grievance mechanisms, collective bargaining agreements.

Box 13. NCP specific instance regarding ING climate risk management and disclosure

National Contact Points for Responsible Business Conduct (NCPs for RBC) are agencies established by governments. Their mandate is twofold: to promote the OECD *Guidelines* and related due diligence guidance, and to handle cases (referred to as "specific instances") as a non-judicial grievance mechanism. To date, 49 governments have established an NCP for RBC.

In recent years, NCP's have also handled cases involving the responsibility of financial practitioners to address climate risks. For example:

In 2017, the NGOs Oxfam Novib, Greenpeace, BankTrack and Friends of the Earth the Netherlands submitted a case to the Dutch NCP concerning ING, a Dutch bank. Specifically, the submitters argued that the bank does not report the levels of GHG emissions caused by its lending activities and has not yet announced whether it intends to do so in the near future. In addition, they argued that the bank has not set a target to reduce GHG emissions in its lending.

In April 2019, the case was concluded, and the parties reached an agreement, in which ING committed to align its portfolio with the Paris Agreement. The parties also recognised ING's adoption of the "Terra" approach towards measuring, target setting and steering the bank's climate impact, using the Paris Agreement Capital Transition Assessment (PACTA) tool developed by 2 Degrees Investing Initiative (2DII), as well as the Partnership for Carbon Accounting Financials (PCAF), as underlying methodologies.

Additionally, ING and the NGOs called directly on the Dutch Government to request the International Energy Agency (IEA) to develop two 1.5 degrees scenarios, with and without the use of Carbon Capture and Storage (CCS), that provide a 66% chance to limit global warming to below 1.5 degrees.

Source: Dutch National Contact Point for Responsible Business Conduct, (2019[102]), Final Statement Dutch NCP specific instance, 4 NGOs versus ING bank, www.oecdguidelines.nl/latest/news/2019/04/19/final-statement-dutch-ncp-specific-instance-4-ngos-versus-ing-bank.

Investors may also wish to establish their own grievance mechanisms although there have been limited examples of this to date. A grievance mechanism can serve as a platform to address potential shortcomings related to an investor's due diligence process. It can also serve as an early warning or feedback mechanism for investors to alert them to certain issues. Some international climate funds and international financial institutions have established grievance mechanisms for projects that have received public funding, which may also be supported by institutional investors. The Green Climate Fund (GCF) for example has established an Independent Redress Mechanism (IRM) to address complaints by people who believe they are negatively affected or may be affected by projects or programmes funded by the Green Climate Fund. More recently, the UNDP-OECD Impact Standards for Financing Sustainable Development (IS-FSD) also recommend donor agencies and development finance institutions to ensure that a functioning grievance mechanism is in place and aligned with RBC principles and standards (OECD/UNDP, 2021[103]).

Conclusion

This chapter identified where additional research and analysis is needed to better inform institutional investors (and other key stakeholders) on assessing, managing and reporting on climate risks and impacts associated with their portfolios and investment decisions.

This tool presents initial technical guidance to help institutional investors implement risk-based due diligence to identify and respond to adverse climate risks and impacts directly linked to their operations, products and services, based on the *OECD Guidelines* and the OECD Due Diligence Guidance for RBC as well as existing practices and tools. This draft guidance can be a useful resource to investors in the context of changing regulatory requirements, market practices and stakeholder expectations.

Although investors have a wealth of existing tools and resources to draw on in carrying out risk assessment for adverse climate impacts, this tool has identified several outstanding gaps and challenges investors may face in carrying out due diligence with respect to climate impacts directly linked to their operations, products and services. In that regard, additional research, analysis and dialogue will be needed to:

- Explore the connections and differences between environmental and financial materiality of climate change, and their implications for metrics, targets, standards, and disclosure frameworks.
- Clarify what appropriate climate mitigation benchmarks and alignment methodologies can be recommended for investors under an RBC due diligence approach, (e.g. climate alignment frameworks).
- Provide guidance on appropriate and viable pathways to help investors meet their climate mitigation objectives and targets at portfolio level and within each asset class.
- Further apply RBC due diligence standards to help enhance the credibility, comparability and tracking of financial sector and real economy net-zero transition commitments; and
- Develop useful metrics, targets and benchmarks related to climate adaptation and resilience, to help investors track climate due diligence performance in terms of climate adaptation and resilience at portfolio and asset class levels.

More broadly, additional dialogue will be needed to consult, engage and inform institutional investors (and other key stakeholders) on assessing, managing and reporting on impacts associated with their portfolios and investment decisions as well as clarifying expectations for investee corporations in relation to due diligence of adverse climate impacts and risks.

References

2° Investing Initiative (2020), *PACTA 2020 Swiss Assessment: 80% of the market assessed in first-of-its kind study of the Swiss financial sector's alignment with climate goals - 2DII*, https://2degrees-investing.org/bridging-the-gap/ (accessed on 14 19 2023). [77]

Ang, G. (2020), *Background paper of the 3 September 2020 workshop on Climate Change: Uncertainties, assumptions and surprises*. [101]

Boffo et al. (2020), *ESG Investing: Environmental Pillar Scoring Reporting*, OECD Publishing, Paris, https://www.oecd.org/finance/esg-investing-environmental-pillar-scoring-and-reporting.pdf. [57]

Carbon 4 (2021), *Our latest Carbon Impact Analytics methodological guide*, https://www.carbon4finance.com/our-latest-carbon-impact-analytics-methodological-guide2 (accessed on 14 September 2023). [41]

Carney, M. (2019), *Remarks given during the UN Secretary General's Climate Action Summit 2019*, https://www.bankofengland.co.uk/speech/2019/mark-carney-remarks-at-united-nations-climate-action-summit-2019 (accessed on 14 September 2023). [76]

Carney, M. (2015), *Breaking the tragedy of the Horizon - climate change and financial stability - speech by Mark Carney*, Speech given at Lloyd's of London, https://www.bankofengland.co.uk/speech/2015/breaking-the-tragedy-of-the-horizon-climate-change-and-financial-stability (accessed on 14 September 2023). [11]

CDP (2023), *CDP Technical Note: Relevance of Scope 3 Categories by Sector*, https://cdn.cdp.net/cdp-production/cms/guidance_docs/pdfs/000/003/504/original/CDP-technical-note-scope-3-relevance-by-sector.pdf. [65]

CDP (2019), *Major risk or rosy opportunity - Are companies ready for climate change?*, https://www.cdp.net/en/research/global-reports/global-climate-change-report-2018/climate-report-risks-and-opportunities (accessed on 14 September 2023). [84]

CDP/WWF (2021), *The CDP-WWF temperature rating methodology*, https://www.cdp.net/en/investor/temperature-ratings/cdp-wwf-temperature-ratings-methodology (accessed on 14 September 2023). [42]

CDSB (2019), *CDSB Framework for reporting environmental and climate change information*, CDSB, https://www.cdsb.net/sites/default/files/climateguidancedoublepage.pdf. [22]

Chiara, E. (2018), *Corporate Responsibility for Climate Change: Litigation and Other Grievance Mechanisms*, Asser Institute Centre for International and European Law, https://www.asser.nl/DoingBusinessRight/Blog/post/corporate-responsibility-for-climate-change-litigation-and-other-grievance-mechanisms-by-elisa-chiaro (accessed on 14 September 2023). [99]

Climate Action 100+ (2023), *Climate action 100+ releases the latest evolution of the net zero company benchmark*, https://www.climateaction100.org/news/climate-action-100-releases-the-latest-evolution-of-the-net-zero-company-benchmark/ (accessed on 14 September 2023). [81]

Climate Action 100+ (2020), *Climate Action 100+ Net Zero Company Benchmark*, https://www.climateaction100.org/net-zero-company-benchmark (accessed on 14 September 2023). [44]

Climate Action Tracker (2023), *Climate Action tracker*, https://climateactiontracker.org/ (accessed on 14 September 2023). [49]

Clyde & Co (2019), *Climate change: Liability risks for businesses, directors and officers*, https://online.flippingbook.com/view/648937/2 (accessed on 14 September 2023). [97]

Clyde & Co (2018), *The rising tide of climate change liability*, https://resilience.clydeco.com/articles/the-rising-tide-of-climate-change-liability (accessed on 14 September 2023). [98]

CRREM (2021), *Carbon Risk Real Estate Monitor*, https://www.crrem.eu/ (accessed on 14 September 2023). [50]

Dobrinevski, A. and R. Jachnik (2020), "Exploring options to measure the climate consistency of real economy investments : The manufacturing industries of Norway", *OECD Environment Working Papers*, No. 159, OECD Publishing, Paris, https://doi.org/10.1787/1012bd81-en. [89]

Dobrinevski, A. and R. Jachnik (2020), "Exploring options to measure the climate consistency of real economy investments: The transport sector in Latvia", *OECD Environment Working Papers*, No. 163, OECD Publishing, Paris, https://doi.org/10.1787/48d53aac-en. [90]

Dutch National Contact Point for Responsible Business Conduct (2019), *Final Statement Dutch NCP specific instance, 4 NGOs versus ING bank*, https://www.oecdguidelines.nl/latest/news/2019/04/19/final-statement-dutch-ncp-specific-instance-4-ngos-versus-ing-bank (accessed on 14 September 2023). [102]

Ehlers, T. (2020), *Green bonds and carbon emissions: exploring the case for a rating system at the firm-level*, https://www.bis.org/publ/qtrpdf/r_qt2009c.pdf. [82]

Equator Principles (2023), *Guidance Note on Climate Change Risk Assessment*, https://equator-principles.com/app/uploads/Guidance-CCRA_May-2023.pdf. [80]

ERCST (2021), *The Role of Supply Chain Emissions in Decarbonization and Compliance*, https://ercst.org/wp-content/uploads/2021/09/20210921-Report_Role-of-Supply-Chain-Emissions-in-Decarbonization-and-Compliance-v17.pdf. [66]

EU Platform on Sustainable Finance (2022), *Final Report on Minimum Safeguards*, https://finance.ec.europa.eu/system/files/2022-10/221011-sustainable-finance-platform-finance-report-minimum-safeguards_en.pdf. [61]

EU TEG (2020), *Taxonomy: Final report of the Technical Expert Group on Sustainable Finance*, https://ec.europa.eu/info/sites/info/files/business_economy_euro/banking_and_finance/documents/200309-sustainable-finance-teg-final-report-taxonomy_en.pdf. [59]

European Commission (2019), *EU taxonomy for sustainable activities*, https://finance.ec.europa.eu/sustainable-finance/tools-and-standards/eu-taxonomy-sustainable-activities_en (accessed on 14 September 2023). [54]

European Commission (2019), *Guidelines on reporting climate-related information*, https://ec.europa.eu/finance/docs/policy/190618-climate-related-information-reporting-guidelines_en.pdf. [23]

European Union (2020), *Regulation (EU) 2020/852 of the European Parliament and of the Council of 18 June 2020 on the establishment of a framework to facilitate sustainable investment*, http://data.europa.eu/eli/reg/2020/852/oj (accessed on 14 September 2023). [58]

FTSE Russell (2021), *Beyond Ratings Data*, https://www.ftserussell.com/beyond-ratings-data (accessed on 14 September 2023). [47]

Germanwatch (2021), *Climate Change Performance Index*, https://germanwatch.org/en/CCPI (accessed on 14 September 2023). [46]

GFANZ (2022), *Guidance on use of Sectoral pathways for financial institutions*, https://assets.bbhub.io/company/sites/63/2021/11/GFANZ-Progress-Report.pdf. [87]

Global Commission on Adaptation (2019), *Adapt Now: A Global Call for Leadership on Climate Resilience*, https://gca.org/reports/adapt-now-a-global-call-for-leadership-on-climate-resilience (accessed on 14 September 2023). [85]

Hallegatte, S. et al. (2020), "From Poverty to Disaster and Back: a Review of the Literature", *Economics of Disasters and Climate Change*, Vol. 4/1, pp. 223-247, https://doi.org/10.1007/s41885-020-00060-5. [17]

I4CE (2019), *Understanding transition scenarios: Eight steps for reading and interpreting these scenarios*, i4CE, https://www.i4ce.org/en/publication/understanding-transition-scenarios-eight-steps-for-reading-and-november-2019-interpreting-these-scenarios/ (accessed on 14 September 2023). [73]

IIGCC (2022), *First net zero guidance for private equity for GPs and LPs*, https://www.iigcc.org (accessed on 14 September 2023). [51]

IIGCC (2022), *Working towards a climate resilience investment framework*, https://www.iigcc.org/resource/working-towards-a-climate-resilience-investment-framework (accessed on 14 September 2023). [27]

IIGCC (2021), *Net Zero Investment Framework 1.5 C - Implementation Guide*, IIGCC, https://www.parisalignedinvestment.org/media/2021/03/PAII-Net-Zero-Investment-Framework_Implementation-Guide.pdf. [37]

IIGCC (2020), *Net Zero Investment Framework for Consultation*, http://www.iigcc.org (accessed on 14 September 2023). [24]

IIGCC (2020), *Understanding physical climate risks and opportunities*, http://www.iigcc.org (accessed on 14 September 2023). [14]

IIGCC (2019), *Navigating climate scenario analysis: A guide for institutional investors*, IIGCC, https://www.iigcc.org/resources/navigating-climate-scenario-analysis-a-guide-for-intuitional-investors (accessed on 14 September 2023). [68]

IIGCC (2015), *Climate Change Investment Solutions: A Guide for Asset Owners*, https://www.iigcc.org (accessed on 14 September 2023). [79]

IPCC (2023), *AR6 Synthesis Report: Climate Change 2023*, https://www.ipcc.ch/report/sixth-assessment-report-cycle (accessed on 14 September 2023). [10]

IPCC (2015), *AR5 Synthesis Report*, https://www.ipcc.ch/report/ar5/syr/synthesis-report (accessed on 14 September 2023). [106]

IPCC (2014), *: Summary for policymakers. In: Climate Change 2014: Impacts, Adaptation, and Vulnerability.*, Cambridge University Press, https://www.ipcc.ch/site/assets/uploads/2018/03/ar5_wgII_spm_en-1.pdf. [13]

Jachnik, R. and A. Dobrinevski (2021), "Measuring the alignment of real economy investments with climate mitigation objectives: The United Kingdom's buildings sector", *OECD Environment Working Papers*, No. 172, OECD Publishing, Paris, https://doi.org/10.1787/8eccb72a-en. [91]

Jachnik, R., M. Mirabile and A. Dobrinevski (2019), "Tracking finance flows towards assessing their consistency with climate objectives", *OECD Environment Working Papers*, No. 146, OECD Publishing, Paris, https://doi.org/10.1787/82cc3a4c-en. [92]

Leiter and Olhoff (2019), *Adaptation metrics - Current Landscape and Evolving Practices*, UNEP, https://www.researchgate.net/publication/336135027_Adaptation_metrics_-_Current_Landscape_and_Evolving_Practices (accessed on 14 September 2023). [56]

Lenton et al. (2019), "Climate tipping points - too risky to bet against", *Nature*, Vol. 575/7784, pp. 592-595, https://doi.org/10.1038/d41586-019-03595-0. [16]

Lenton et al. (2008), "Tipping elements in the Earth's climate system", *Proceedings of the National Academy of Sciences of the United States of America*, Vol. 105/6, pp. 1786-1793, https://doi.org/10.1073/pnas.0705414105. [15]

Marjanac et al. (2017), "Acts of god, human influence and litigation", *Nature Geoscience*, Vol. 10/9, pp. 616-619, https://doi.org/10.1038/ngeo3019. [94]

Monasterolo, I. (2019), "Climate Change and the Financial System", https://ssrn.com/abstract=3479380 (accessed on 14 September 2023). [12]

Moody's Investors Service (2016), *Moody's Approach to Climate Risk*, https://climate.moodys.com/ (accessed on 14 September 2023). [53]

MSCI (2021), *Implied Temperature Rise*, https://www.msci.com/our-solutions/climate-investing/implied-temperature-rise#:~:text=What%20is%20Implied%20Temperature%20Rise%20(ITR)%3F,funds%20with%20global%20temperature%20goals. (accessed on 14 September 2023). [43]

MSCI (2021), *MSCI and Burgiss launch Carbon Footprinting of Private Equity and Debt Funds to assess impact of climate change on private asset portfolios*, https://www.msci.com/documents/10199/dd786a40-dbb6-4218-da01-3d2e3d0a5907. [52]

NGFS (2020), *Guide to climate scenario analysis for central banks and supervisors*, https://www.ngfs.net/en/guide-climate-scenario-analysis-central-banks-and-supervisors (accessed on 14 September 2023). [75]

NGFS (2020), *NGFS Climate Scenarios for central banks and supervisors*, https://www.ngfs.net/en/ngfs-climate-scenarios-central-banks-and-supervisors (accessed on 14 September 2023). [74]

Ninety One (2021), *Ninety One launches the Net Zero Sovereign Index*, https://ninetyone.com/en/newsroom/ninety-one-launches-the-net-zero-sovereign-index (accessed on 14 September 2023). [48]

Noels, J. and R. Jachnik (2022), "Assessing the climate consistency of finance: taking stock of methodologies and assessing their links to climate mitigation policy objectives", *OECD Environment Working Papers*, No. 200, OECD Publishing, Paris, https://doi.org/10.1787/d12005e7-en. [2]

NZAOA (2022), *UN-convened Net-Zero Asset Owner Alliance Target Setting Protocol*, NZAOA, https://www.unepfi.org/net-zero-alliance/resources/target-setting-protocol-second-edition (accessed on 14 September 2023). [28]

NZDPU (2022), *Development of the Net-Zero Data Public Utility*, https://assets.bbhub.io/company/sites/71/2022/11/development-of-the-net-zero-data-public-utility-november-2022.pdf. [67]

OECD (2023), *G20/OECD Principles of Corporate Governance*, OECD Publishing, Paris, https://doi.org/10.1787/9789264236882-en. [34]

OECD (2023), *OECD Guidelines for Multinational Enterprises*, OECD Publishing, Paris, https://doi.org/10.1787/9789264115415-en. [8]

OECD (2022), *Climate Change and Corporate Governance, Corporate Governance*, OECD Publishing, Paris, https://doi.org/10.1787/272d85c3-en. [78]

OECD (2022), *Climate Tipping Points: Insights for Effective Policy Action*, OECD Publishing, Paris, https://doi.org/10.1787/abc5a69e-en. [18]

OECD (2022), *Climate Tipping Points: Insights for Effective Policy Action*, OECD Publishing, Paris, https://doi.org/10.1787/abc5a69e-en. [105]

OECD (2022), *OECD Guidance on Transition Finance: Ensuring Credibility of Corporate Climate Transition Plans*, Green Finance and Investment, OECD Publishing, Paris, https://doi.org/10.1787/7c68a1ee-en. [19]

OECD (2021), *Research Collaborative on Tracking Finance for Climate Action*, https://www.oecd.org/env/researchcollaborative (accessed on 14 September 2023). [88]

OECD (2021), *The role of OECD instruments on responsible business conduct in progressing environmental objectives*, OECD Publishing, Paris, https://mneguidelines.oecd.org/The-role-of-OECD-instruments-on-responsible-business-conduct-in-progressing-environmental-objectives.pdf. [6]

OECD (2020), *Developing Sustainable Finance Definitions and Taxonomies*, Green Finance and Investment, OECD Publishing, Paris, https://doi.org/10.1787/134a2dbe-en. [60]

OECD (2020), *Green Infrastructure in the Decade for Delivery: Assessing Institutional Investment*, Green Finance and Investment, OECD Publishing, Paris, https://doi.org/10.1787/f51f9256-en. [36]

OECD (2020), "Nature-based solutions for adapting to water-related climate risks", *OECD Environment Policy Papers*, No. 21, OECD Publishing, Paris, https://doi.org/10.1787/2257873d-en. [86]

OECD (2019), *Accelerating Climate Action: Refocusing Policies through a Well Being Lens - Highlights*, OECD Publishing, Paris, https://www.oecd.org/environment/cc/Highlights-Accelerating-Climate-Action-Refocusing-Policies-through-a-Well-being-Lens.pdf. [64]

OECD (2019), *Biodiversity: Finance and the Economic and Business Case for Action*, OECD Publishing, Paris, https://doi.org/10.1787/a3147942-en. [31]

OECD (2018), *Climate Resilient Infrastructure*, OECD Publishing, Paris, https://doi.org/10.1787/23097841. [55]

OECD (2018), *OECD Due Diligence Guidance for Responsible Business Conduct*, OECD Publishing, Paris, https://mneguidelines.oecd.org/OECD-Due-Diligence-Guidance-for-Responsible-Business-Conduct.pdf. [5]

OECD (2017), *Investment governance and the integration of environmental, social and governance factors*, OECD Publishing, Paris, https://www.oecd.org/finance/Investment-Governance-Integration-ESG-Factors.pdf. [3]

OECD (2017), *Responsible business conduct for institutional investors: Key considerations for due diligence under the OECD Guidelines for Multinational Enterprises*, OECD Publishing, Paris, https://mneguidelines.oecd.org/RBC-for-Institutional-Investors.pdf. [7]

OECD (2013), *High-level principles of long-term investment financing by institutional investors*, OECD Publishing, Paris, https://www.oecd.org/finance/private-pensions/G20-OECD-Principles-LTI-Financing.pdf. [35]

OECD (2012), *Greenhouse gas emissions and the potential for mitigation from materials management within OECD countries*, OECD Publishing, Paris, https://www.oecd.org/env/waste/50034735.pdf. [21]

OECD (2006), *OECD Guidelines on Pension Fund Asset Management. Recommendation of the Council*, OECD Publishing, Paris, https://legalinstruments.oecd.org/en/instruments/OECD-LEGAL-0341 (accessed on 14 September 2023). [107]

OECD/CDSB (2015), *Climate change disclosure in G20 countries: Stocktaking of corporate reporting schemes*, OECD Publishing, Paris, https://www.oecd.org/daf/inv/mne/Report-on-Climate-change-disclosure-in-G20-countries.pdf. [20]

OECD/UNDP (2021), *The Impact Standards for Financing Sustainable Development*, OECD Publishing, Paris, https://doi.org/10.1787/d571f17c-en. [103]

Patalano, R. (2020), *ESG Investing: Practices, Progress and Challenges*, OECD Publishing, Paris, https://www.oecd.org/finance/ESG-Investing-Practices-Progress-Challenges.pdf. [9]

PCAF (2022), *The Global GHG Accounting and Reporting Standard for the Financial Industry*, https://carbonaccountingfinancials.com/en/standard#the-global-ghg-accounting-and-reporting-standard-for-the-financial-industry (accessed on 14 September 2023). [38]

Röttgers et al. (2018), *OECD Progress Update on Approaches to Mobilising Institutional Investment for Sustainable Infrastructure*, OECD Publishing, Paris, https://doi.org/10.1787/45426991-en. [83]

S&P Global (2021), *Climate Change Physical Risk dataset*, https://www.marketplace.spglobal.com/en/datasets/trucost-paris-alignment-(186) (accessed on 14 September 2023). [40]

Sabin Center for Climate Change Law (2020), *U.S. Climate Change Litigation*, US Climate Change Litigation, http://climatecasechart.com/us-climate-change-litigation/ (accessed on 14 September 2023). [96]

SBTi (2021), *Financial Institutions*, https://sciencebasedtargets.org/sectors/financial-institutions#about-the-project (accessed on 14 September 2023). [29]

Setzer and Byrnes (2019), *Global trends in climate change litigation: 2019 snapshot*, Grantham Institute, https://www.lse.ac.uk/granthaminstitute/publication/global-trends-in-climate-change-litigation-2020-snapshot/ (accessed on 14 September 2023). [93]

Tandon, A. (2021), *Transition finance: Investigating the state of play. A stocktake of emerging approaches and financial instruments*, OECD Publishing, Paris, https://doi.org/10.1787/68becf35-en. [62]

TCFD (2020), *2020 Status Report: Task Force on Climate-related Financial Disclosures - Financial Stability Board*, https://www.fsb.org/2020/10/2020-status-report-task-force-on-climate-related-financial-disclosures/ (accessed on 14 September 2023). [104]

TCFD (2019), *Task Force on Climate-related Financial Disclosures: Status Report*, https://www.tcfdhub.org/resource/task-force-on-climate-related-financial-disclosures-2019-status-report/ (accessed on 14 September 2023). [70]

TCFD (2017), *Recommendations of the Task Force on Climate-related Financial Disclosures (TCFD), Final Report*, https://www.fsb-tcfd.org/wp-content/uploads/2017/06/FINAL-2017-TCFD-Report-11052018.pdf. [33]

TCFD (2017), *Technical Supplement: The Use of Scenario Analysis in Disclosure of Climate-Related Risks and Opportunities*, TCFD, https://www.tcfdhub.org/scenario-analysis/ (accessed on 14 September 202). [69]

The Shift Project for AFEP (2019), “Energy and Climate Scenarios: Evaluation and guidance”, https://theshiftproject.org/en/article/energy-climate-scenarios-evaluation-guidance-report/ (accessed on 14 September 2023). [72]

TNFD (2023), *TNFD v0.4 Beta Release*, https://framework.tnfd.global/ (accessed on 14 September 2023). [63]

Transition Pathway Initiative (2021), *The TPI tool*, https://www.transitionpathwayinitiative.org/ (accessed on 14 September 2023). [39]

UN HLEG (2022), *Integrity Matters: Net Zero Commitments by Businesses, Financial Institutions, Cities and Regions*, https://www.un.org/sites/un2.un.org/files/high-level_expert_group_n7b.pdf. [4]

UN PRI (2016), *How asset owners can drive responsible investments: Beliefs, Startegies and Mandates*, https://www.unpri.org/asset-owner-resources/investment-beliefs-examples-from-practice/288.article (accessed on 14 September 2023). [30]

UNEP (2021), *Global Climate Litigation Report: 2020 Status Review*, https://www.unep.org/resources/report/global-climate-litigation-report-2020-status-review (accessed on 14 September 2023). [95]

UNEP (2016), *Lenders and Investors Environmental Liability: How Much is Too Much?*, https://wedocs.unep.org/20.500.11822/7521. [100]

UNEP FI (2019), *Changing Course: A comprehensive investor guide to scenario-based methods for climate risk assessment, in response to the TCFD*, UNEP, https://www.unepfi.org/industries/investment/changing-course-a-comprehensive-investor-guide-to-scenario-based-methods-for-climate-risk-assessment-in-response-to-the-tcfd (accessed on 14 September 2023). [71]

UNEP FI/PRI (2020), *UN-convened Net-Zero Asset Owner Alliance*, https://www.unepfi.org/net-zero-alliance (accessed on 14 September 2023). [25]

UNFCCC (2015), *The Paris Agreement*, UNFCCC, https://unfccc.int/process-and-meetings/the-paris-agreement (accessed on 14 September 2023). [1]

WBCSD (2019), *Business Climate Resilience*, https://www.wbcsd.org/eg3zf (accessed on 14 September 2023). [26]

WEF (2019), *How to Set Up Effective Climate Governance on Corporate Boards Guiding principles and questions*, https://www3.weforum.org/docs/WEF_Creating_effective_climate_governance_on_corporate_boards.pdf. [32]

World Benchmarking Alliance (2021), *Climate and Energy Benchmark*, https://www.worldbenchmarkingalliance.org/climate-and-energy-benchmark (accessed on 14 September 2023). [45]

Annex A. Relationship of OECD RBC due diligence expectations to existing initiatives

This Annex includes tables comparing steps and recommendations of OECD RBC due diligence expectations to those of selected existing initiatives and frameworks related to climate risk management for investors. The initiatives and frameworks below were selected on the basis of the size of their membership or degree of uptake. This initial stocktake of existing initiatives and frameworks may be adapted or added to over time to reflect additional initiatives or frameworks with broad uptake across institutional investors. The objective of this Annex is to provide investors with a simple reference point to assess to which extent initiatives and frameworks they may already be a part of or be implementing meet expectations of the OECD RBC due diligence process. In addition to the below, there are a significant amount of disclosure frameworks providing guidance and expectations on reporting and measurement of climate impacts and performance. In addition to the tables included in this Annex, Table 1 in the main body of this report provides an overview of how leading disclosure frameworks on climate compare to public reporting expectations of the OECD RBC due diligence framework.

Box A A.1. Brief overview of selected climate-related frameworks and initiatives for investors

The Task Force on Climate-related Financial Disclosures (TCFD): The TCFD was created by the Financial Stability Board (FSB) in December 2015. It followed a request by the G20 to FSB in April 2015, to design a set of recommendations to encourage climate-related financial disclosure by both financial and non-financial institutions and assess the type of information that should be released to shift financial flows towards a low-carbon economy. The TCFD framework has gained momentum and is increasingly being implemented by several institutional investors worldwide. The TCFD recommendations primarily focus on the financial materiality of climate change, while the RBC due diligence approach and the present tool consider the social and environmental impacts of climate change. However, the TCFC also requires the consideration of forward-looking climate scenarios, which encourage investors to think beyond short-term financially material climate risks. Furthermore, the structure of the TCFD disclosure recommendations (on governance, strategy, risk management, metrics and targets) are closely related to key steps of RBC due diligence approach.

The Net Zero Investment Framework: The Paris Aligned Investment Initiative (PAII) was established in 2019 by the Institutional Investors Group on Climate Change (IIGCC). The IIGCC is the European membership body for investor collaboration on climate change, with more than 270 members, mainly pension funds and asset managers, across 16 countries with over EUR 35 trillion in assets under management. The PAII provides recommendation to help institutional investors align their portfolios with the Paris Agreement objectives and thus consider the environmental materiality lens. In August 2020, the IIGCC released a Net Zero Investment Framework for consultation, as part of the PAII, to explore how investors can align their portfolios with the goals of the Paris Agreement. The IIGCC launched the Net Zero Investment Framework in March 2021.

Climate Action 100+: Launched in 2017 at the One Planet Summit, Climate Action 100+ is an investor-led initiative that aims to ensure that the world's largest corporate GHG emitters take necessary action to mitigate climate change impacts. The common engagement agenda includes three commitments or "three asks" of participating investors: 1) to implement strong governance frameworks, 2) to reduce GHG emissions across the value chain and 3) to provide enhanced corporate disclosure in line with the TCFD recommendations. These commitments are related to several steps of the due diligence process. Additionally, the focus on the Paris Agreement's goal of limiting global average temperature (with the move towards net-zero emissions by 2050 or sooner) highlights that this initiative also considers environmental materiality of climate change.

Source: TCFD, (2017[33]), Recommendations of the Task Force on Climate-related Financial Disclosures (TCFD), Final Report, www.fsb-tcfd.org/wp-content/uploads/2017/06/FINAL-2017-TCFD-Report-11052018.pdf; TCFD, (2020[104]), 2020 Status Report: Task Force on Climate-related Financial Disclosures - Financial Stability Board, www.fsb.org/2020/10/2020-status-report-task-force-on-climate-related-financial-disclosures; IIGCC, (2020[24]), Net Zero Investment Framework for Consultation, www.iigcc.org; IIGCC, (2021[37]), Net Zero Investment Framework 1.5 C - Implementation Guide, www.parisalignedinvestment.org/media/2021/03/PAII-Net-Zero-Investment-Framework_Implementation-Guide.pdf; Climate Action 100+, (2020[44]), Climate Action 100+ Net Zero Company Benchmark, www.climateaction100.org/net-zero-company-benchmark.

Annex Table 1. Measure 1: Embed climate considerations into policies and management systems.

RBC due diligence sub-measures	TCFD	Climate Action 100+	Net Zero Investment Framework
Adopting policies on climate:	Requires disclosure regarding: - Climate governance, strategy, risk management (from a financial materiality perspective), and metrics/targets set.	Requires disclosure regarding: – Decarbonisation strategy, governance of climate risks/opportunities, capital alignment and climate policy support.	- Recognises the importance of setting climate objectives as part of policy objectives. - Aligns with the Net Zero Asset Owner Alliance and provides framework on which investors can define strategies, objectives and measure alignment at 3 levels: portfolio level (Governance, Portfolio Reference Targets, SAA), Asset class level (Asset class alignment) and external level (Policy advocacy, Engagement).
	No explicit mention of: - Inclusion of climate objectives into investment mandates, policies or charters. Financial materiality focus for risk-management.	No explicit mention of: - Climate objectives into investment mandates, policies or charters.	
Embedding climate considerations into management systems through: - 1) embedding climate considerations at a board level - 2) and management level - 3) ensuring functional alignment and - 4) ensuring sufficient resources.	Recommends disclosures related to: - How climate related issues are reported to the board (frequency, method, organisational structure etc.). - Responsibility assignment for climate-related risk assessments to management positions and how they fit into organisations' financial reporting processes.	Recommends: - Implementation of a strong governance framework which clearly articulates the board's accountability and oversight of climate change risk. - Inclusion of members appointed and responsible specifically for climate issues in executive committees. - Disclosure of organisational structures by which management is informed about climate-related issues. - Integrating responsibility for climate issues sustainability	Recommends: - Strengthening board oversight of climate risks, impacts and direction for action. - IIGCC framework to integrate management of climate risks into all key processes (including governance, strategy, policy advocacy, engagement strategies, and financial planning over short, medium and long term.) - Communication of incentives related to climate. - Extending climate issue beyond the remit of sustainability departments.

RBC due diligence sub-measures	TCFD	Climate Action 100+	Net Zero Investment Framework
		departments. - Disclosure on how climate risks are incorporated into strategic and financial planning in short, medium, long term.	
	No explicit mention of: - Requirements or recommendations regarding board composition. - Incentives for management of climate risks. - Recruitment and selection of investment managers. -Resources.	No explicit mention of: - Requirements or recommendations regarding board composition. - Recruitment and selection of investment managers. - Resources.	No explicit mention of: - Requirements or recommendations regarding board composition. - Assigning climate responsibilities to executive and management level positions. - Clarifying organisation structures and reporting lines on climate issues including to boards. - Recruitment and selection of investment managers. - Resources.

Sources: Authors compilation and analysis; based on TCFD, (2017[33]), Recommendations of the Task Force on Climate-related Financial Disclosures (TCFD), Final Report, www.fsb-tcfd.org/wp-content/uploads/2017/06/FINAL-2017-TCFD-Report-11052018.pdf; Climate Action 100+, (2020[44]), Climate Action 100+ Net Zero Company Benchmark, www.climateaction100.org/net-zero-company-benchmark; IIGCC, (2020[24]), Net Zero Investment Framework for Consultation, www.iigcc.org; IIGCC, (2021[37]), Net Zero Investment Framework 1.5 C - Implementation Guide, www.parisalignedinvestment.org/media/2021/03/PAII-Net-Zero-Investment-Framework_Implementation-Guide.pdf.

Annex Table 2. Measure 2. Identify and assess actual and potential adverse climate impacts.

RBC due diligence sub-measures	TCFD	Climate Action 100+	The Net Zero Investment Framework
1) Identifying and assessing climate risks, impacts and opportunities at portfolio level **2) Identifying and assessing climate risks, impacts and opportunities asset level and.** **3) Prioritising the most significant risks and impacts for further action.**	Recommends disclosure of: - Carbon foot printing information. - All processes by which climate risks and impacts are assessed. - How climate risks identification and assessment in integrated into investment decision making processes. - Climate-related risks and impacts the organisation has identified over the short, medium and long term. Recommends both historical and forward looking (scenario) analyses when considering the potential impacts of climate. - Climate-related opportunities the organisation has identified over the short, medium and long term - How climate-related risks and opportunities are prioritised.	Recommends: - Carbon footprint and other GHG emissions footprint across investment types and asset classes be assessed and disclosed. - How climate risks identification and assessment in integrated into investment decision making processes. - Climate risks and opportunities be prioritised and how such prioritisation decisions are made should be disclosed. - Both historical and forward looking (scenario) analyses when considering the potential impacts of climate change in line with TCFD.	Recommends: - Screening portfolios to identify climate-related risks and impacts. - Climate financial risk assessment be undertaken line with TCFD recommendations. -Estimating the carbon footprint and other GHG emissions footprint for overall portfolio emission target. - Assessment building on existing work, processes or requirements of investors. - How climate risks identification and assessment in integrated into investment decision making processes. - Scenario analysis and forward looking approaches to ensure SAA asset class return expectations are informed by a realistic assessment of climate risks and opportunities or to stress test potential portfolios. - Sectors most material to climate change and impacts be identified and prioritised using NACE classification codes as well as weighted carbon intensity. - Stakeholder and market engagement to facilitate alignment. - Screening portfolios to identify climate-related opportunities.
	No explicit mention of: - Identification of adaptation	No explicit mention of: - Working with investment advisors and	No explicit mention of: - Assessing existing and potential assets

RBC due diligence sub-measures	TCFD	Climate Action 100+	The Net Zero Investment Framework
	and resilience measures (or lack thereof). - Stakeholder engagement. Focus is on transition and physical risks from a financial materiality perspective.	managers to understand how they assess climate risks and impacts. - Assessing existing and potential assets for climate mitigation, adaptation and resilience. - Stakeholder engagement. - Identifying investment opportunities. Focus is on transition and physical risks from a financial materiality perspective.	for climate mitigation, adaptation and resilience.

Sources: Based on TCFD, (2017[33]), Recommendations of the Task Force on Climate-related Financial Disclosures (TCFD), Final Report, www.fsb-tcfd.org/wp-content/uploads/2017/06/FINAL-2017-TCFD-Report-11052018.pdf; Climate Action 100+, (2020[44]), Climate Action 100+ Net Zero Company Benchmark, www.climateaction100.org/net-zero-company-benchmark; IIGCC, (2020[24]), Net Zero Investment Framework for Consultation, www.iigcc.org; IIGCC, (2021[37]), Net Zero Investment Framework 1.5 C - Implementation Guide, www.parisalignedinvestment.org/media/2021/03/PAII-Net-Zero-Investment-Framework_Implementation-Guide.pdf.

Annex Table 3. Measure 3. Seek to prevent and mitigate adverse climate impacts.

RBC due diligence sub-measures	TCFD	Climate Action 100+	The Net Zero Investment Framework
1) Responding to climate considerations at portfolio level **2) Taking climate considerations into account in portfolio allocation at asset class-level** **3) Influencing existing assets through engagement**	Recommends disclosure of: - The impact of financial planning on acquisitions and divestments from carbon-intensive assets. - Increased diversification in financial assets to capture new opportunities through investing in greenfield and resilient infrastructure (low carbo energy production, energy efficiency, grid connectivity etc.).	Recommends: - That companies may consider divestment from carbon-intensive sectors and communicate about these. - Increasing diversification in financial assets to capture opportunities in low-carbon, greenfield and resilient infrastructure. - Increasing engagement, in multi-stakeholder initiatives for asset managers and corporations to better manage risks.	Recommends: - Aligning portfolios with climate objectives through Strategic Asset Allocation. - Undertaking a cross-section analysis of climate-related opportunities and mapping those against SAA targets in place. - That companies consider divestment from carbon-intensive sectors to reduce portfolios' exposure to emissions intensive assets. - Increasing investments in appropriate low carbon opportunities such as renewable energy, energy efficiency, low-carbon transportation, energy storage and energy efficiency buildings or energy efficiency technologies. - Increasing engagement, active ownership and engagement in multi-stakeholder initiatives. - Engagement and stewardship to a foster emission reduction by favouring transitioning assets.
	No explicit mention of: - Strategic asset allocation - Engagement, active ownership and stewardship.	No explicit mention of: - Strategic asset allocation - Stewardship and active ownership or the way engagement can influence existing assets.	

Sources: Based on TCFD, (2017[33]), Recommendations of the Task Force on Climate-related Financial Disclosures (TCFD), Final Report, www.fsb-tcfd.org/wp-content/uploads/2017/06/FINAL-2017-TCFD-Report-11052018.pdf; Climate Action 100+, (2020[44]), Climate Action 100+ Net Zero Company Benchmark, www.climateaction100.org/net-zero-company-benchmark; IIGCC, (2020[24]), Net Zero Investment Framework for Consultation, www.iigcc.org; IIGCC, (2021[37]), Net Zero Investment Framework 1.5 C - Implementation Guide, www.parisalignedinvestment.org/media/2021/03/PAII-Net-Zero-Investment-Framework_Implementation-Guide.pdf.

Annex Table 4. Measure 4. Tracking implementation and results

RBC due diligence sub-measures	TCFD	Climate Action 100+	The Net Zero Investment Framework
1) Developing targets and benchmarks to track climate performance at a portfolio, asset class and asset-level. **2) Tracking performance against benchmarks and target.**	Recommends reporting on: - Climate targets and performance against those targets. - Metrics related to weighted carbon intensity.	Recommends: - Setting a series of targets to move towards next-zero emission by 2050 or sooner.	Recommends: - Setting targets and objectives both at portfolio and asset-level and reporting on: - Emissions Intensity Reduction Goal and a <10 Reference Target (CO_2 Emissions Intensity); or a reference target for absolute CO_2 emission reduction. - Initial goals for allocation to climate solutions representing a percentage of revenues or capex from AUM. - Supplementing SAA objectives with climate-related objectives (carbon intensity and allocation to climate solutions). Recommends tracking: - Climate performance based on weighted carbon or GHG intensity. - Carbon footprint at a portfolio level to set a reference target for total, absolute emissions reduction. - Reduction in exposure to climate related assets.
	Does not explicitly require target setting related to: - Emissions - Revenue, assets, liability and capital allocation of carbon-intensive assets. - Forward-looking transition-oriented metrics. - Climate resilience and adaptation.	Does not explicitly require target setting related to: - Emissions - Revenue, assets, liability and capital allocation of carbon-intensive assets. - Forward-looking transition-oriented metrics. - Climate resilience and adaptation. Any specific metrics for measuring progress against targets are not identified.	Does not explicitly require specific target setting related to: - Liability and capital allocation of carbon-intensive assets. - Forward-looking transition-oriented metrics. - Climate resilience and adaptation.

Sources: Based on TCFD, (2017[33]), Recommendations of the Task Force on Climate-related Financial Disclosures (TCFD), Final Report, www.fsb-tcfd.org/wp-content/uploads/2017/06/FINAL-2017-TCFD-Report-11052018.pdf; Climate Action 100+, (2020[44]), Climate Action 100+ Net Zero Company Benchmark, www.climateaction100.org/net-zero-company-benchmark; IIGCC, (2020[24]), Net Zero Investment Framework for Consultation, www.iigcc.org; IIGCC, (2021[37]), Net Zero Investment Framework 1.5 C - Implementation Guide, www.parisalignedinvestment.org/media/2021/03/PAII-Net-Zero-Investment-Framework_Implementation-Guide.pdf.

Annex Table 5. Measure 5. Communicate how impacts are addressed

RBC due diligence sub-measures	TCFD	Climate Action 100+	The Net Zero Investment Framework
Communicate publicly on: - Investor climate policy, including due diligence approaches. - Information on measures taken to embed climate issues into policies and management systems, and across asset classes. - Report on investors' identified areas of significant climate risks and impacts, the significant adverse climate impacts and risks identified, prioritised and assessed.	Recommends disclosure of: - Governance processes with respect to climate risks and opportunities. - Climate-related risks and opportunities where such information is material and relevant to the business strategy. - Process for identification, assessment and management of climate-related risks, including prioritisation criteria. - Metrics used, scope 1-3 emissions and related-GHG risk.	Aligned with TCFD recommendations.	Aligned with TCFD recommendations.

RBC due diligence sub-measures	TCFD	Climate Action 100+	The Net Zero Investment Framework
- The risk management and other tools used to assess and prioritise climate risks and impacts. - The actions taken to prevent or mitigate those risks including relevant investment strategies considered or adopted across asset classes, engagement activities undertaken by the investor etc. - Investors' future climate plans, metrics and targets, and; - Where possible estimated timelines and benchmarks for improvement and their outcomes. - Measures to track implementation and results.	- Targets used to manage climate risks and performance against such targets.		
	Not explicitly mentioned: - Investor climate policy, including due diligence approaches - Specific actions taken to prevent or mitigate climate risks including relevant investment strategies considered or adopted across asset classes, engagement activities undertaken by the investor etc. Climate risks, impacts and management strategy considered from a financial materiality perspective.	Aligned with TCFD recommendations.	Aligned with TCFD recommendations.

Note: See also Table 1 in core report comparing due diligence reporting expectations with leading disclosure frameworks.
Source: Authors compilation and analysis; based on TCFD, (2017[33]), Recommendations of the Task Force on Climate-related Financial Disclosures (TCFD), Final Report, www.fsb-tcfd.org/wp-content/uploads/2017/06/FINAL-2017-TCFD-Report-11052018.pdf; Climate Action 100+, (2020[44]), Climate Action 100+ Net Zero Company Benchmark, www.climateaction100.org/net-zero-company-benchmark; IIGCC, (2020[24]), Net Zero Investment Framework for Consultation, www.iigcc.org; IIGCC, (2021[37]), Net Zero Investment Framework 1.5 C - Implementation Guide, www.parisalignedinvestment.org/media/2021/03/PAII-Net-Zero-Investment-Framework_Implementation-Guide.pdf.

Annex Table 6. Measure 6. Provide for or co-operate in remediation if appropriate.

RBC due diligence sub-measures	TCFD	Climate Action 100+	The Net Zero Investment Framework
- Engagement in remediation, litigation, and dialogue related to climate impacts. For example, through co-operation with judicial or state-based non judicial mechanism. - Establishment of operational-level grievance mechanisms	Not explicitly addressed.	Not explicitly addressed.	Not explicitly addressed.

Sources: Authors compilation and analysis; based on TCFD, (2017[33]), Recommendations of the Task Force on Climate-related Financial Disclosures (TCFD), Final Report, www.fsb-tcfd.org/wp-content/uploads/2017/06/FINAL-2017-TCFD-Report-11052018.pdf; Climate Action 100+, (2020[44]), Climate Action 100+ Net Zero Company Benchmark, www.climateaction100.org/net-zero-company-benchmark; IIGCC, (2020[24]), Net Zero Investment Framework for Consultation, www.iigcc.org; IIGCC, (2021[37]), Net Zero Investment Framework 1.5 C - Implementation Guide, www.parisalignedinvestment.org/media/2021/03/PAII-Net-Zero-Investment-Framework_Implementation-Guide.pdf.

Notes

[1] Within the framework of laws, regulations and administrative practices in the countries in which they operate, and in consideration of relevant international agreements, principles, objectives, and standards. (OECD, 2023[8]).

[2] Investors can ***contribute*** to adverse climate impacts through their own activities when greenhouse gas emissions or impacts on carbon sinks associated with these activities are inconsistent with internationally agreed global temperature goals based on best available science, including as assessed by the Intergovernmental Panel on Climate Change (IPCC). Whether an investor has introduced and implemented science-based policies, strategies and transition plans on climate change mitigation and adaptation in line with the recommendations of the *OECD Guidelines* is relevant in this regard (OECD, 2023[8]).

[3] The portfolio emissions of global financial institutions are on average over 700 times larger than direct emissions and represents over 99% of total scope 1, 2 and 3 reported emissions by the financial service sector (CDP, 2023[65]).

[4] "According to this approach, universal owners hold a 'slice' of the whole global economy and market through their portfolios. They can therefore improve their long-term financial performance by acting in such a way as to encourage healthy and stable economies and markets. This will ensure that they can pay benefits to their beneficiaries but also provides collateral benefits to the wider community (OECD, 2017[3]).

[5] As discussed in the previous section I, this tool also builds on the *OECD Due Diligence Guidance for Responsible Business Conduct,* which sets out a common framework for due diligence processes across all sectors (OECD, 2018[5]).

[6] The Environment chapter of the *OECD Guidelines* states that "*in consideration of relevant international agreements, principles, objectives, and standards, enterprises should conduct their activities in a manner that takes due account of the need to protect the environment.*" (OECD, 2023[8]).

[7] For instance, in the European Union, to mean net-zero emissions by 2050 and a 50-55% reduction by 2030, consistent with the commitments under the EU Green Deal.

[8] Such as health, education, jobs, as well as wider environmental quality and resources (OECD, 2019[64]); in addition to human rights.

[9] The Environment chapter of the *OECD Guidelines* explicitly refers to the "establishment of measurable objectives and, where appropriate, targets for improved environmental performance" (OECD, 2023[8]).

[10] Investment beliefs can include ethical beliefs, including for instance exclusion policies. Investment governance is defined as "[t]he set of policies that sets out the investment beliefs, assumptions and

objectives of the investor, and the way in which the organisation is structured in order to implement these policies when investments are made (OECD, 2017[3]).

[11] The Taskforce on Nature-related Financial Disclosures (TNFD) Nature-Related Risk & Opportunity Management and Disclosure Framework v0.4 Beta Release includes a risk and opportunity assessment approach (or LEAP approach), which helps investors (and corporate) manage and disclose evolving nature-related risks. The LEAP approach mirrors and draws in part some of the six-step framework of the RBC due diligence process, including when it comes to engaging with rightsholders (TNFD, 2023[63]).

[12] The EU Taxonomy regulation clarifies that: 1."An economic activity shall qualify as contributing substantially to climate change adaptation where that activity: (a) includes adaptation solutions that either substantially reduce the risk of the adverse impact of the current climate and the expected future climate on that economic activity or substantially reduce that adverse impact, without increasing the risk of an adverse impact on people, nature or assets; or (b) provides adaptation solutions that [...] contribute substantially to preventing or reducing the risk of the adverse impact of the current climate and the expected future climate on people, nature or assets, without increasing the risk of an adverse impact on other people, nature or assets." And 2. "An economic activity shall qualify as contributing substantially to climate change mitigation where that activity contributes substantially to the stabilisation of greenhouse gas concentrations in the atmosphere at a level which prevents dangerous anthropogenic interference with the climate system consistent with the long-term temperature goal of the Paris Agreement through the avoidance or reduction of greenhouse gas emissions or the increase of greenhouse gas removals, including through process innovations or product innovations." (European Union, 2020[58]).

[13] Including carbon dioxide (CO_2), methane (CH_4), nitrous oxide (N_2O) and fluorinated gases [hydrofluorocarbons (HFCs), perfluorocarbons (PFCs), sulphur hexafluoride (SF_6) and nitrogen trifluoride (NF_3)].

[14] The subsequent section discusses outstanding challenges to measure and estimate emissions of investee corporations and invested assets, including scope 3 emissions. Section on "Measure 4: Track implementation and results" e metrics and targets across asset classes.

[15] The warming of the climate system is unequivocal (IPCC, 2015[106]). Human influence on the climate system is also clear (IPCC, 2015[106]).

[16] e.g. linked to uncertainties about the transient climate response (including uncertainties in radiative processes and climate feedbacks), the carbon cycle, and equilibrium climate sensitivity.

[17] Noting that these should also be assessed to ensure that methodologies applied to label a product as "green" are credible and consistent with and investors own climate policies and objectives.

[18] i.e. the long-term asset mix over the main investment categories; (OECD, 2006[107]).

[19] Generally considered to refer to assets or organisations with relatively high direct or indirect GHG emissions; (TCFD, 2017[33]).

[20] See for example the EU Corporate Sustainability Reporting Directive (CSRD) and upcoming European Sustainability Reporting Standards (ESRS). See also Regulation (EU) 2019/2088 on sustainability-related disclosures in the financial services sector (or SFDR).

www.ingramcontent.com/pod-product-compliance
Lightning Source LLC
Chambersburg PA
CBHW061225240926
51846CB00006B/1356
* 9 7 8 9 2 6 4 3 9 4 9 6 4 *